UNDERSTANDING SCIENCE & NATURE

Transportation

TIME-LIFE
ALEXANDRIA, VIRGINIA

CONTENTS

1
Riding the Changing Rails

The train is one of the great engineering triumphs of modern life. Since the mid-1800s, railroads have served as a reliable, efficient means of moving people and cargo overland. The earliest trains *(top),* driven by steam power, played an important role in the success of the Industrial Revolution in England. In the United States, the Baltimore and Ohio Railroad began operating in 1830. Ten years later, coal-fired steam trains were hauling passengers and freight over some 2,800 miles of track. By 1860 the nation's rail lines covered over 30,000 miles, and railroads were playing a key role in moving settlers into the West.

In the 1940s the Union Pacific Railroad built the Big Boys, the most powerful steam locomotives ever. These monsters could hit 75 miles per hour and haul 4,000-ton loads up steep slopes in the Rocky Mountains. Today, diesel-powered locomotives *(second from top)* pull most freight trains in the United States, whereas electric engines are used widely in Europe. Commuters worldwide travel to and from work in electric-powered railcars *(middle),* each containing its own electric motor. High-speed bullet trains *(second from bottom)* can hit 186 miles per hour. In the future, the experimental maglev train *(bottom),* which would float in the air over magnetic track, could travel as fast as 300 miles per hour.

From the Rocket *(top left),* the world's most powerful train in 1829, to today's experimental magnetic levitation train *(bottom),* railroads have come to move large numbers of people and great amounts of freight quickly and cheaply.

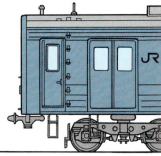

What Keeps a Train on Its Tracks?

Trains today may be bigger, faster, and more powerful than the first trains of 160 years ago, but they still have the same flanged iron wheels rolling on I-shaped iron rails. Every train wheel has a 1-inch lip, or flange, extending from its inner rim. This flange guides the train's wheels along the rail and around curved tracks. The flange and rail system produces so little fric-

Flange
Rail joint
Rail
Fish plate
Spring clip
Track spike
Wood crosstie

Elastic rail support

A rail sits on wood or concrete ties buried in a gravel bed. Usually, long bolts passing through spring clips hold the rail in place. This elastic system makes for a smoother train ride.

Rail joint

In jointed track, a gap between 39-foot rails allows steel rails to expand when hot. A bolted joint bar holds the segmented rails together. Today, most main-line rail is welded together.

Traction

A locomotive's weight forces its wheels to grip the smooth rail, providing the traction that pulls a train along the track and up inclines.

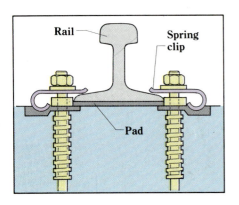

Rail
Spring clip
Pad

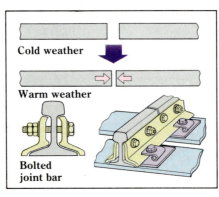

Cold weather
Warm weather
Bolted joint bar

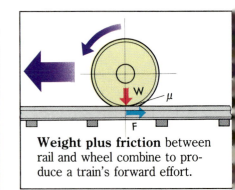

Weight plus friction between rail and wheel combine to produce a train's forward effort.

tion that if a 40-ton train car rolling at 60 miles per hour lost its power, it would travel 5 miles before stopping. In contrast, a 40-ton truck would roll about 1 mile before stopping.

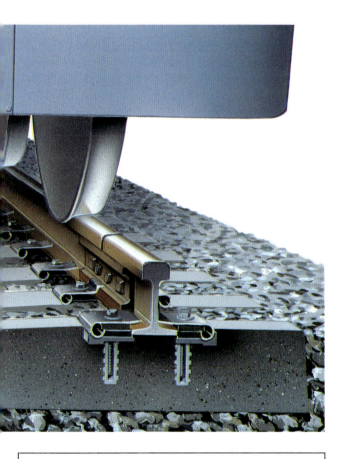

Making the curves

A train passing through a curve experiences a force, known as centrifugal force, that pulls it toward the outside of the curve. To fight this sideways force, the outside rail is raised above the inside rail. This elevation, or cant, enables trains to keep their speed through curves.

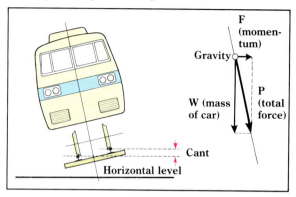

Slack

The distance between rails is greater in curves than on straight sections of track. This reduces the friction on the train's wheels as the train pulls to the outside and reduces wear on the rails.

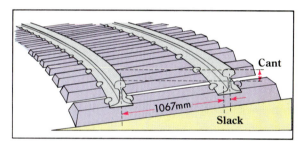

Switching tracks

Moving a train from one track to another requires shifting its wheels with movable switch rails. Guardrails allow the wheels to cross the "frog point" where the rails meet. A train passing the switch below will take the straight right-hand track.

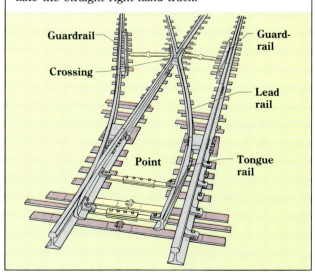

Wheel trucks

A train car's wheels are mounted on trucks, movable platforms that also hold the car's suspension system. Each truck, with two pairs of wheels, swivels on a center plate, giving flexibility as a train passes through a curve. The independent suspension helps to ensure a smoother ride.

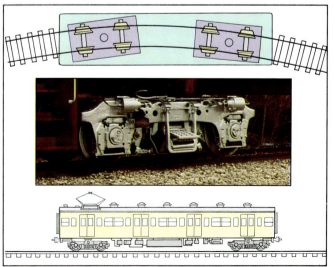

How Are Train Cars Hooked Together?

The life of a train is one of additions and subtractions: Add a few cars at one place; remove a few at another. What makes this possible is the automatic coupling mechanism, a device that locks train cars together securely, yet can unlock easily with a yank on a release lever. Couplers come in several forms. Subway trains and light-rail vehicles use contact couplers, which provide a secure, smooth ride. Knuckle-type couplers, resembling two hands clasped together by the fingers, are common on railroad trains. A rotary-shank coupler allows freight cars to turn upside down and dump their loads without being uncoupled from the train.

Automatic couplings

The standard train coupling works like clasped hands. As two cars approach, the fingers are open. When the fingers collide, they close upon each other and a lock drops into place. To open the coupling, the cars are pushed together and the release lever is lifted by hand.

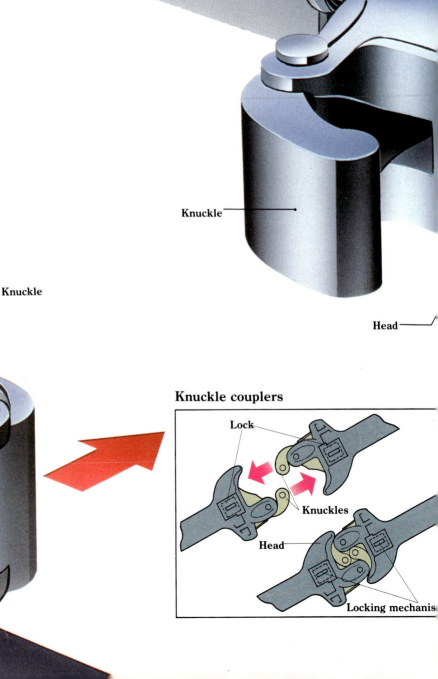

Release lever

Knuckle

Head

Knuckle

Knuckle couplers

Lock

Knuckles

Head

Locking mechanis

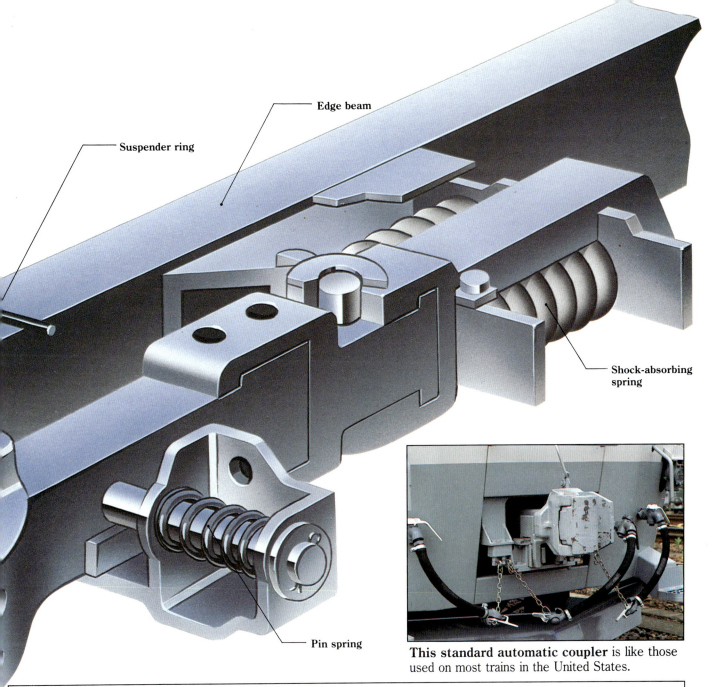

Suspender ring

Edge beam

Shock-absorbing spring

Pin spring

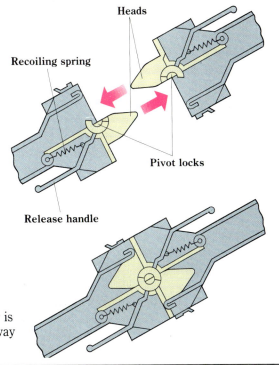

This standard automatic coupler is like those used on most trains in the United States.

Contact couplers

When the heads of two contact couplers meet side by side, they cause a pivot lock to fall into place. Pulling on the release handles releases the recoiling springs, unlocking the coupling. Contact couplings form a tighter joint than the knuckle-type automatic coupler, reducing the jolts between cars when the train starts or stops. Contact couplings also have automatic connections for air-brake and electrical lines.

Heads

Recoiling spring

Pivot locks

Release handle

The contact coupler is standard on most subway and elevated trains.

Are Train Brakes Safe?

The most critical safety system on a train has to be its brakes. Since 1900 all American freight trains have used the automatic air brake, a complex system of hoses, compressors, valves, and couplings that will bring a train 150 cars long safely to a stop. Since its invention in 1872, nearly every part of the automatic air-brake system has been improved, but the basic operating principle remains unchanged: Compressed air pushes on a piston, which forces a brake shoe against the train's wheels *(right)*. The resulting friction stops the train. The system is called automatic because the brakes go on automatically whenever there is a break in the air lines. Today's air brakes can even sense whether a train is empty or heavily loaded and apply the correct amount of braking in either case.

Electric commuter trains have a different type of brake that uses electromagnetic resistance instead of friction to stop a wheel's motion. These brakes can stop a relatively light commuter train quickly and smoothly, but they would not be able to stop a heavier freight or locomotive-drawn passenger train.

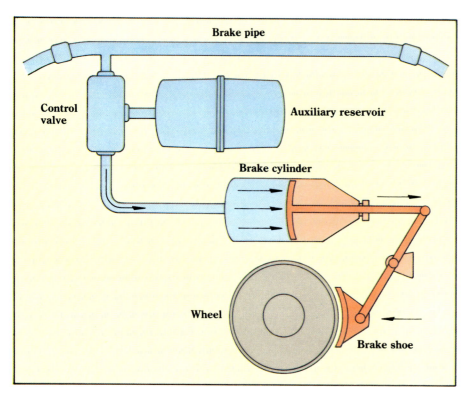

Automatic air brakes in action

When the engineer activates the brake valve (shown in the greatly simplified diagram at left), compressed air passes from the brake pipe into the control valve and on to the brake cylinder. The pressure of the air in the brake cylinder moves levers that press brake shoes against the wheels. Releasing the brake valve allows air pressure to escape from the brake cylinder, and the brake shoe moves away from the wheel.

The control valve also triggers the brakes automatically if a car becomes separated from the rest of the train. An auxiliary reservoir holds extra compressed air to be used in such emergencies.

Electric air brakes

Passenger trains *(below)* use an electronic control circuit to control the amount of air pressure acting on the brake cylinder *(right)*. This system allows for smoother braking than automatic air brakes can provide.

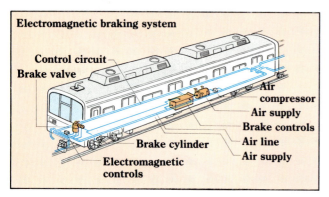

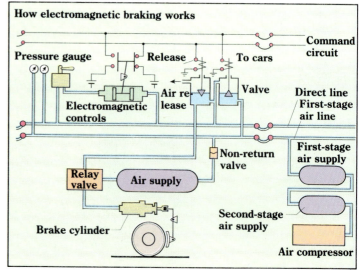

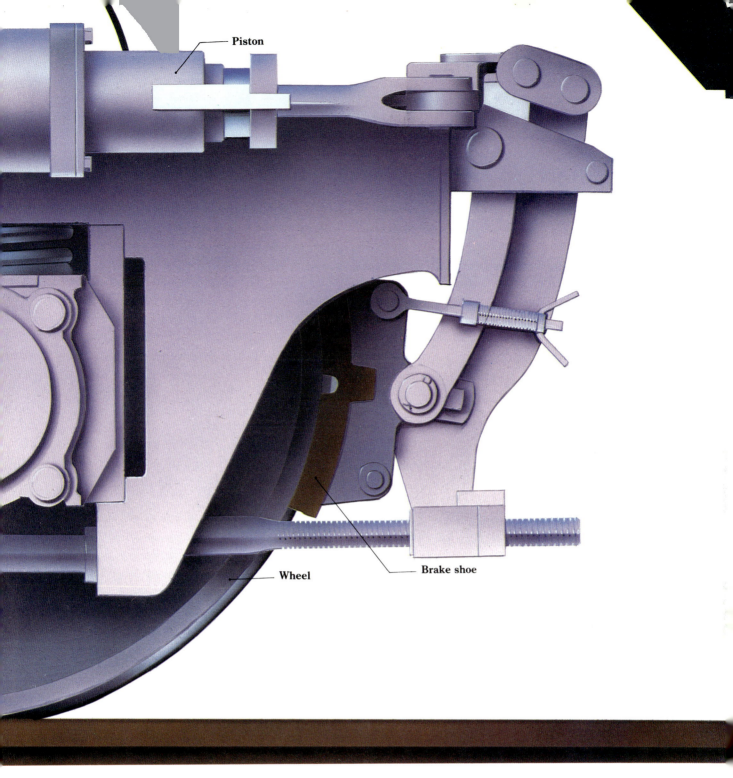

Piston

Wheel

Brake shoe

Electromagnetic brakes

The brakes on an electric commuter train use magnetic resistance instead of friction to provide steady braking control at any speed. Turning off the power to the electric drive motor produces a magnetic field that opposes the rotation of the train's wheels. The longer the power is off, the stronger the braking action.

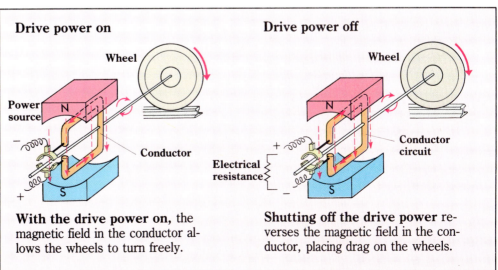

Drive power on

Wheel

Power source

N

Conductor

S

With the drive power on, the magnetic field in the conductor allows the wheels to turn freely.

Drive power off

Wheel

N

Conductor circuit

Electrical resistance

S

Shutting off the drive power reverses the magnetic field in the conductor, placing drag on the wheels.

11

How Do Commuter Train Doors Work?

One of the hallmarks of the modern commuter train is its several sets of automatic sliding doors. Upon arriving at a station, a crew member throws the door-opening switch. This activates a piston-driven gear cog under each pair of doors along one side of the train. The doors on the other side do not open. When the gear cog moves, it slides a door control lever and opens the doors *(below)*. On some trains, a light goes on above each door on the outside of the car. When all the passengers have cleared the doorways, the crew member activates the door-closing switch. The gear cog moves in the opposite direction and the doors slide shut.

With the doors shut, a lock prevents them from opening accidentally. A safety mechanism keeps the train from moving unless all the doors are securely locked. If a door remains ajar, the light over that door remains lit, and the crew member can see which door needs attention.

Normally, the power to operate the doors comes from the same source that runs the train. If the power should fail, an on-board battery pack takes over and can open the doors.

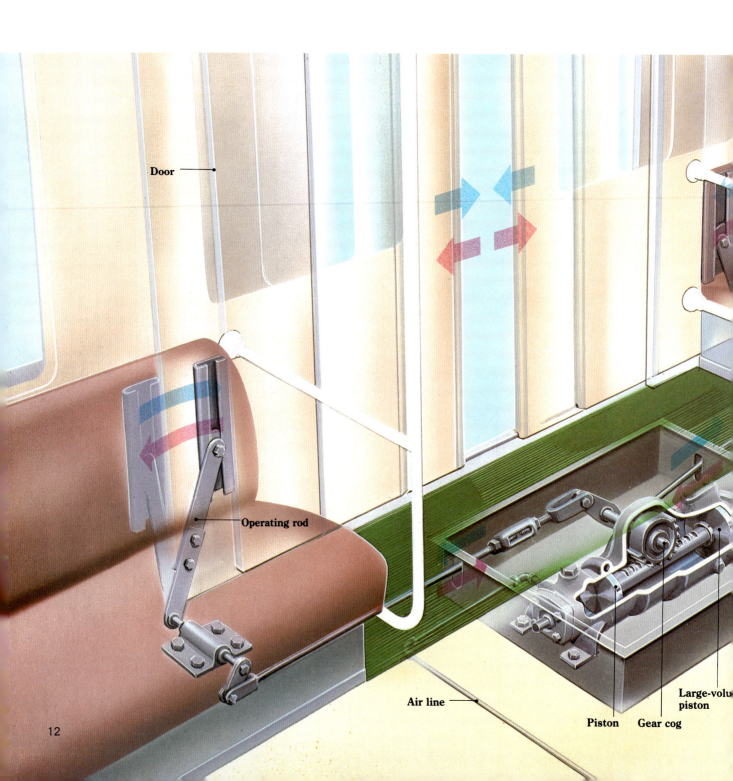

Door

Operating rod

Air line

Piston   Gear cog

Large-volume piston

Single and double doors

A single door *(below, left)* hangs by small wheels from a track. A lever on the door-closing mechanism moves a bar that opens and closes the door. In a double-door system *(below, right)*, a belt and pulley system connects the two doors. When the lever pushes or pulls one door, the other door moves in the opposite direction at the same time.

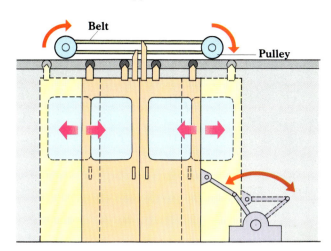

Hanging door wheel

Door-moving lever

Door closer

Belt

Pulley

Opening the doors

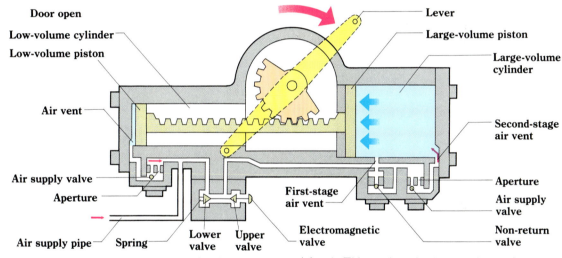

Door open
Low-volume cylinder
Low-volume piston
Air vent
Air supply valve
Aperture
Air supply pipe   Spring   Lower valve   Upper valve

Lever
Large-volume piston
Large-volume cylinder
Second-stage air vent
Aperture
Air supply valve
Non-return valve

First-stage air vent
Electromagnetic valve

Door control lever

When the train operator throws the door-opening switch, a series of valves allow compressed air to enter the large-volume cylinder *(above)*. This pushes the large-volume piston, which moves the gear cog and turns the lever. The doors connected to the lever slide open.

Closing the doors

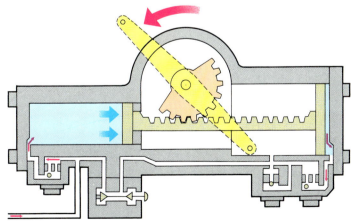

The train operator throws the door-closing switch, which redirects compressed air from the large-volume cylinder to the low-volume cylinder. The low-volume piston moves the gear cog, turning the lever. The doors close.

Red lights signal open doors.

What Were Early Trains Like?

In 1804 a steam-powered locomotive pulled a load of iron through a Welsh ironworks and opened the age of the railroads. Twenty-five years later, British engineer George Stephenson built the Rocket, a steam locomotive with a revolutionary design. When the Liverpool and Manchester Railroad held a contest to pick the best locomotive of the day, the Rocket won the £500 prize. The Liverpool and Manchester line became a success, starting a long period of railroad construction across Europe and the United States.

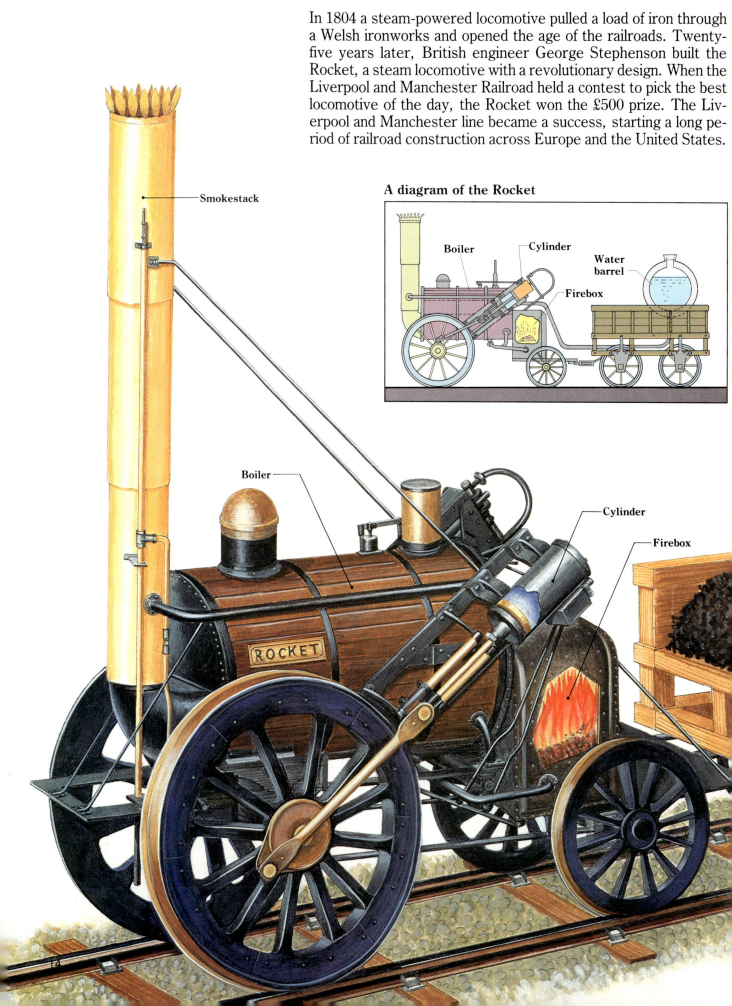

Smokestack

A diagram of the Rocket

Boiler

Cylinder

Water barrel

Firebox

Boiler

Cylinder

Firebox

ROCKET

The Rocket

The Rocket *(below)* had three main parts: the locomotive, which carried the steam boiler and drive cylinders; the firebox, where the coal burned; and the tender, which carried fuel and water. Steam from the boiler powered two large cylinders, one connected to each of the locomotive's front wheels *(right)*. The Rocket's firebox and boiler design made it the first truly practical locomotive and led to the success of the early railroads.

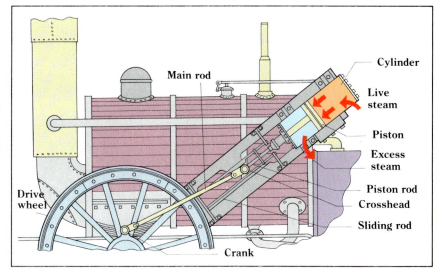

Piston-powered drive wheel

Steam enters the top of the cylinder, forcing the piston downward. This moves the two rods and turns the crank on the wheel. Steam then enters the bottom of the cylinder, pushing the piston back up, which pulls the rods and turns the wheel further.

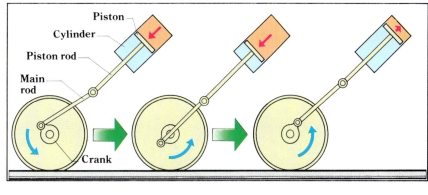

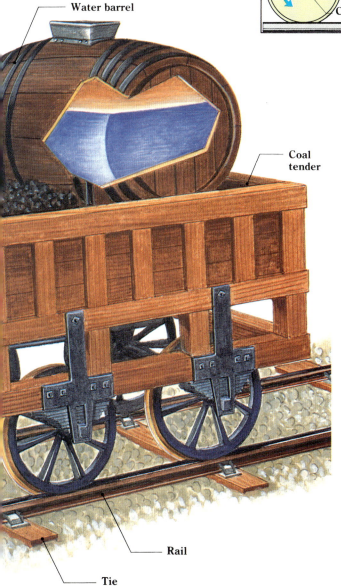

Other early steam locomotives

English engineer Richard Trevithick built the first steam locomotive. In 1804 it hauled 10 tons of iron for 10 miles.

The Locomotion, built in England in 1825, was the first locomotive to run on a public railroad. It was unreliable and offered few advantages over a horse-drawn train.

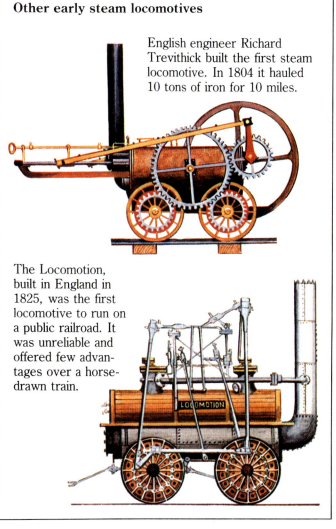

How Does a Steam Locomotive Work?

The steam locomotive uses the energy in high-pressure steam to drive a series of pistons connected directly to the train's wheels by connector rods *(below)*. Its relatively simple design and reliability made the steam locomotive the train of choice from the time of the first locomotives in the early 1800s until after World War II, and it is still used widely in India and China. The steam locomotive's main drawback was its low efficiency—even in the best steam locomotive, only about 6 percent of the energy produced by burning coal is converted into motion.

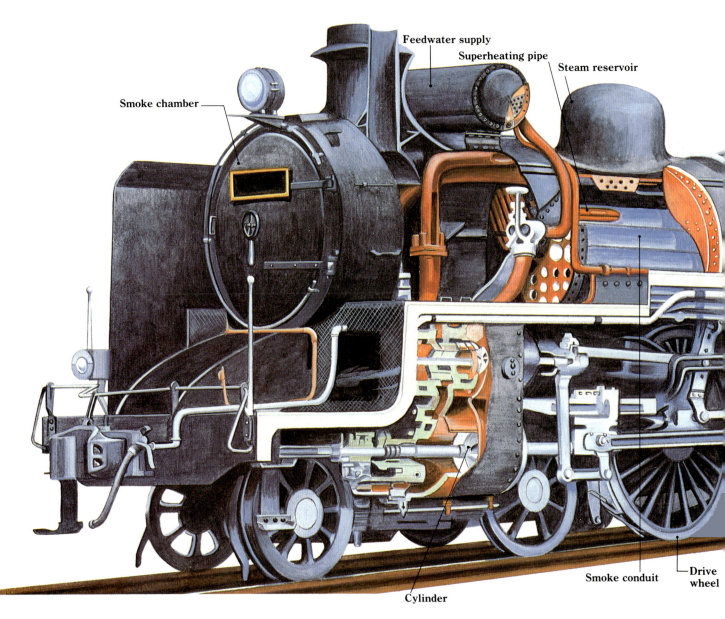

Feedwater supply
Superheating pipe
Steam reservoir
Smoke chamber
Smoke conduit
Drive wheel
Cylinder

The steam locomotive

In a modern steam engine, coal feeds automatically from the tender into the firebox. There, it burns at a temperature close to 2,550° F. Water, also stored in the tender, gets heated twice by the boiler, turning into high-temperature, high-pressure steam. It then passes through the cylinders, moving the pistons and driving the train. Some of the steam condenses back to water and returns to the boiler. The rest of the steam billows from the smokestack.

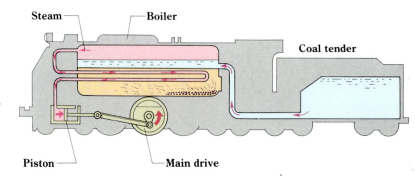

Steam
Boiler
Coal tender
Piston
Main drive

Heat conservation

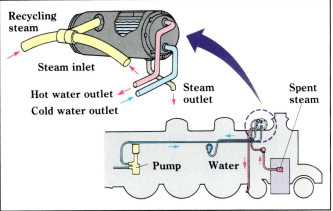

Steam that has passed through the pistons is still hot. In some trains, some of that spent steam is used to preheat cold water before it enters the boiler.

Raising the temperature

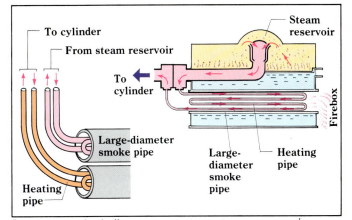

In a water-tube boiler, warm water enters a reservoir surrounding the firebox and turns to steam. The steam then travels through pipes inside the firebox.

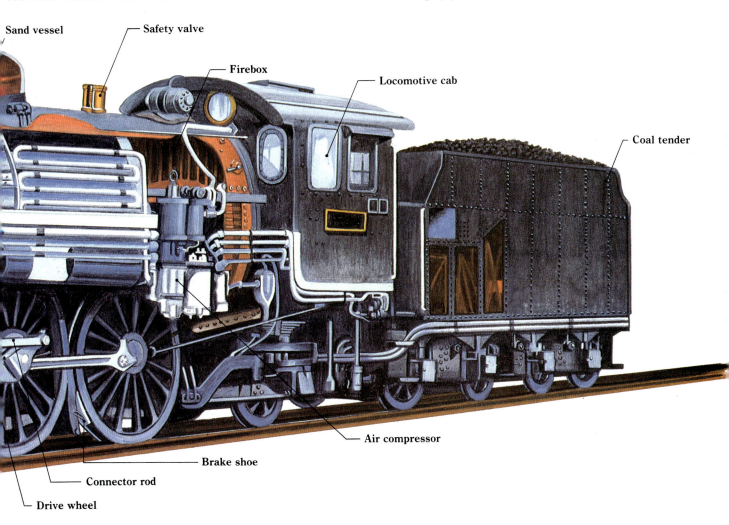

Sand vessel — Safety valve

Firebox

Locomotive cab

Coal tender

Air compressor

Brake shoe

Connector rod

Drive wheel

The steam-driven piston

The piston's left valve opens, admitting high-pressure steam (1). This forces the piston to the right and turns the wheel (2). The left valve closes and the right valve opens, admitting steam on the other side of the piston (3). This forces the piston back to its starting point and drives the wheel to complete one revolution (4). The cycle is ready to begin again.

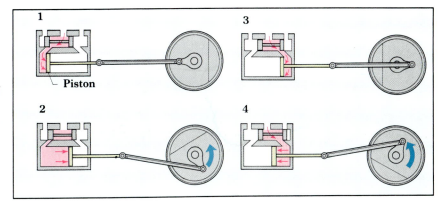

1

Piston

2

3

4

What Is Special on a Luxury Train?

The great American railroad tycoon James J. Hill once commented, "A passenger train is neither useful nor ornamental." Evidently, he had never ridden on the Santa Maria, a train car so luxurious that its builder, the Pullman Palace Car Company, exhibited it at the World's Columbian Exposition of 1893. Soon afterward, George Mortimer Pullman's name became synonymous with luxury, and American passenger trains were known worldwide for their deluxe features.

Today's luxury trains, such as Europe's Orient Express and Japan's Twilight Express *(below)*, re-create the comfortable atmosphere of those glory days of railroading. The simplest rooms have televisions and other amenities, while the deluxe rooms are as comfortable and private as rooms in fine hotels. The suite at the end of the Twilight Express is like a small apartment, with separate rooms for sleeping and sitting.

Japan's Twilight Express prepares to depart the Osaka train station. It will cover the 900 miles to Sapporo in 21 hours.

The Twilight Express

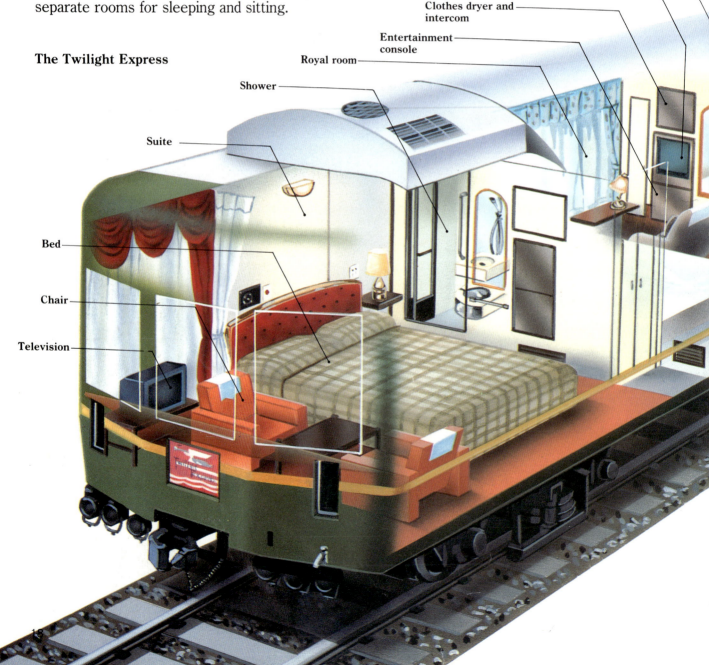

Mirror

Television

Clothes dryer and intercom

Entertainment console

Royal room

Shower

Suite

Bed

Chair

Television

Royal rooms on the Twilight Express have a shower, a television, and a sofa bed.

The suite has a bedroom, complete bathroom, and its own observation room.

The dining car on a luxury train features gourmet cuisine.

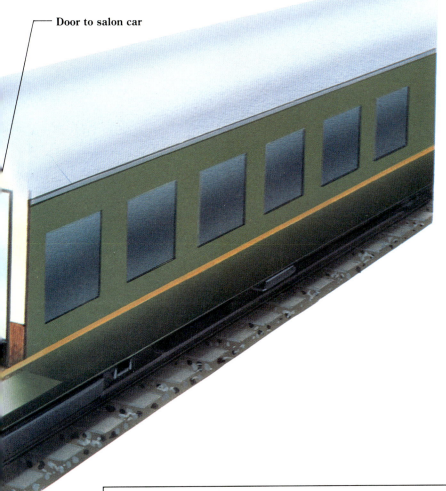

Door to salon car

Passengers can relax in comfort in the salon car.

The salon car shower is for those not traveling in a suite.

The Orient Express

Perhaps the most fabled train in history is the Orient Express, Europe's premier luxury train. Its accommodations rival those of the best first-class hotels, featuring private staterooms, a bar car, and a dining room serving four-star cuisine, all decorated in a luxurious turn-of-the-century style.

A private stateroom

The dining car

How Do Signals Control Trains?

A train, unlike a car or truck, cannot stop quickly when it meets a slower train on the track ahead. Nor can it swerve out of the way to avoid another train stopped at an upcoming station. To avoid collisions between trains running on the same tracks, railroads have developed signaling systems that serve as early-warning devices for train operators.

In the first days of railroading, trains were simply dispatched far enough apart from each other to avoid collisions. Later, railroads switched to the safer distance-interval system: A train could not enter a specific block of track until it was empty. Early signaling systems consisted of flags or lit lamps, which railroads eventually replaced with the colored-light system still used today. In 1872 the first automatic train stop system was installed—a warning or stop signal engaged a train's brakes even if the operator had fallen asleep at the controls.

Automatic block signals

A battery delivers current through a block of track. When a train reaches that block *(bottom)*, the current moves through its wheel. The signal for that block turns red.

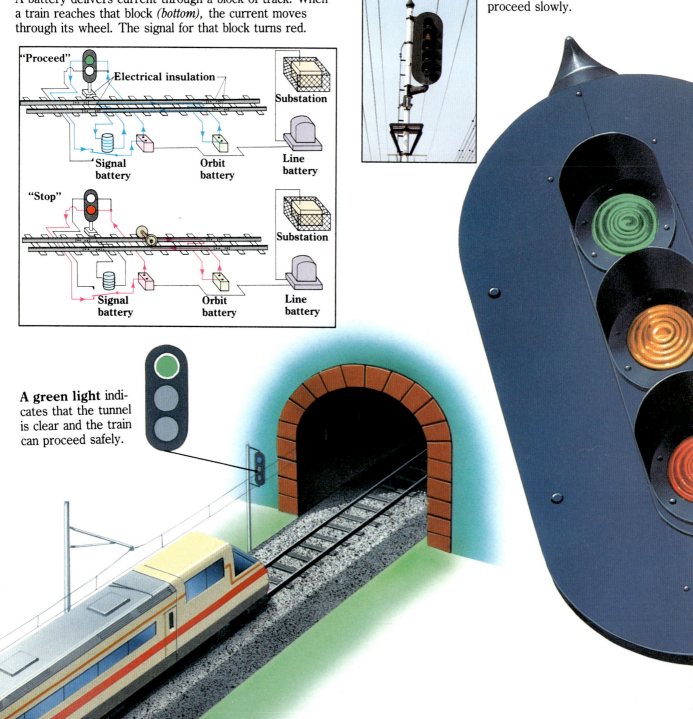

A yellow light on a five-light signal *(left)* tells the engineer to proceed slowly.

A green light indicates that the tunnel is clear and the train can proceed safely.

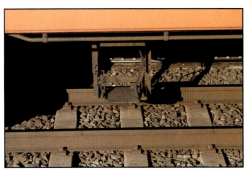

The automatic train stop mounted beneath a railcar will trigger the brakes automatically if it does not receive a clear signal from a transmitter on the tracks.

The green signal indicates clear track ahead.

A red light warns that a train is directly ahead.

A yellow signal warns that a train is two blocks ahead.

A transmitter attaches to the tracks.

● **Automatic train stop system**

When a train (1) approaches a yellow or red signal light without slowing down or stopping (2), a sensor on the track triggers a warning device in the train cab (3). The train operator must press a forestalling lever within a few seconds or the automatic train stop (ATS) system will apply the brakes (4). ATS systems are used on subway systems and in heavily traveled areas of the country.

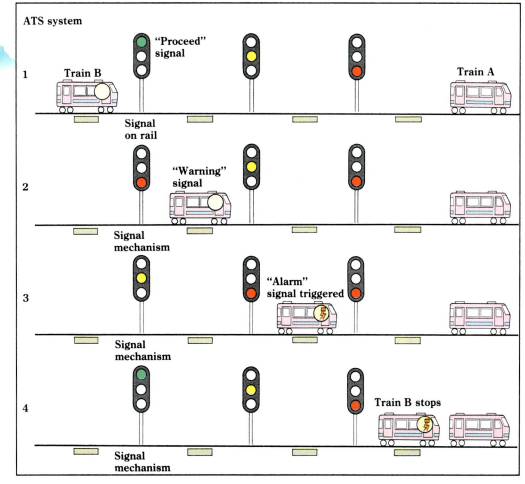

ATS system

1 — Train B / "Proceed" signal / Train A / Signal on rail

2 — "Warning" signal / Signal mechanism

3 — "Alarm" signal triggered / Signal mechanism

4 — Train B stops / Signal mechanism

What Does a Train's Snowplow Do?

When railroad tracks are buried under a heavy blanket of snow, trains may be unable to pass. In parts of the world where snow is common, specially fitted locomotives act as snowplows, clearing the tracks and keeping the trains running. Snowplows such as the single-bladed Jordan plow or the double-bladed Russell plow merely use the locomotive's power to push snow off the tracks. In areas where snowfall is heavy, such as Russia, Scandinavia, northern Japan, and the mountains of the United States, diesel- or electric-powered rotary snowplows use spinning blades to throw snow off the tracks.

The powerful plow wheel creates a brilliant white plume as it throws snow clear of the track.

Rotary snowplow

Plow shield

Plow wheel

Blade wheel

Snow-blowing channel

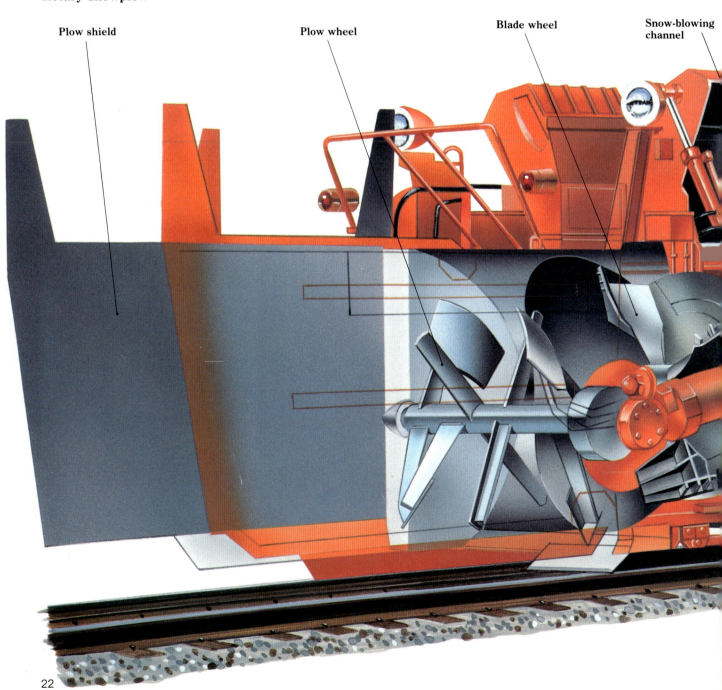

Plow wheel operation

The rotary snowplow looks like an enormous snow blower. Plow shields scrape the snow from either side of the track into the path of the locomotive. The rotating blade whisks the snow into the plow and through the snow-blowing channel, or runner.

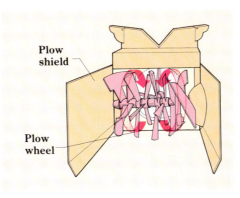

Plow shield

Plow wheel

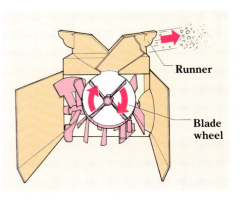

Runner

Blade wheel

The plow shields funnel snow into the spinning blade wheels.

Snow blows from the runner into a ditch next to the track.

Locomotive cab

The snowplow leaves clear track in its wake, making it safe for regular trains to pass through snowy territory.

Other types of snowplows

In areas where snowfall is light, simpler snowplows find use. These bladed plows depend on the locomotive's pushing force to move snow.

A Russell plow shoves snow to the side.

A Jordan plow works like a snow shovel.

What Is an Automatic Train?

Computer-controlled commuter trains carry millions of people daily in cities around the world. While human operators still run most of these trains, they could not do so without computers working together to ensure that the trains run quickly and safely. And in a few rail systems, such as in San Francisco's Bay Area Rapid Transit system and at the Dallas-Fort Worth Airport in Texas, computers run the trains, too. People merely monitor the computers' performance. In the future, fully automated systems may help to relieve the congestion that plagues many big cities.

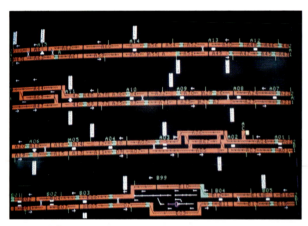

A screen at Washington, D.C.'s Metrorail control room shows track *(orange)* and trains *(white)*.

Staffers in Metrorail's central control room watch train movement on overhead computer screens.

Pneumatic tire

Guide wheel

On-board computer

Automatic operation system

Three types of computers tell automatic commuter trains when to start, stop, and open their doors. The central computer keeps track of train schedules, passing information on to local wayside computers. The wayside computers monitor a train's position and speed and send operating commands to the computer on each train.

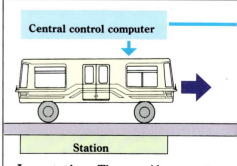

Central control computer

Station

In a station. The wayside computer checks the track for traffic. The track is clear, so it signals the on-board computer to start the train.

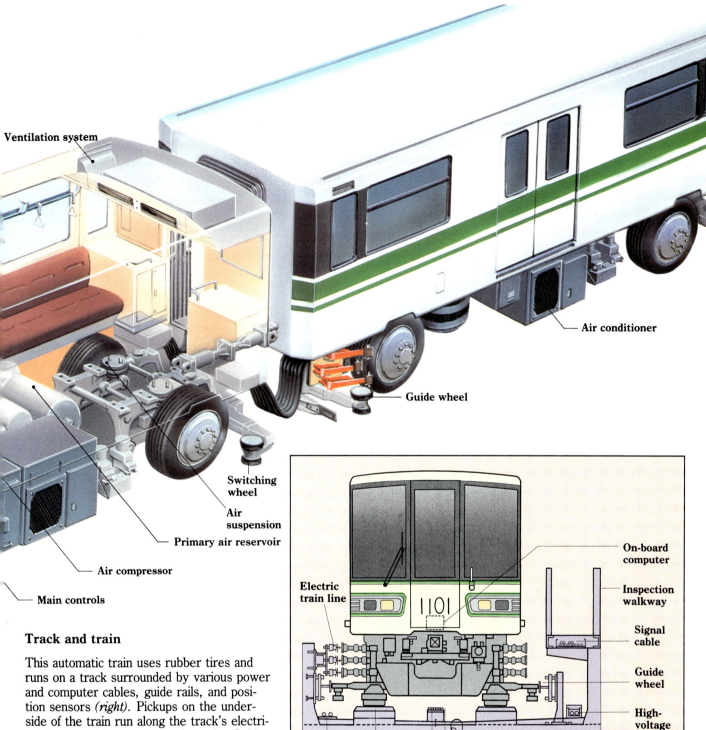

Ventilation system

Air conditioner

Guide wheel

Switching wheel

Air suspension

Primary air reservoir

Air compressor

Main controls

Electric train line

Power cable   Track   Loop line

On-board computer

Inspection walkway

Signal cable

Guide wheel

High-voltage power cable

Track and train

This automatic train uses rubber tires and runs on a track surrounded by various power and computer cables, guide rails, and position sensors *(right)*. Pickups on the underside of the train run along the track's electrical line, providing power to the train. Guide wheels on the cars roll inside a guide rail, keeping the train on a steady course. The loop line monitors the train's position for the wayside computers.

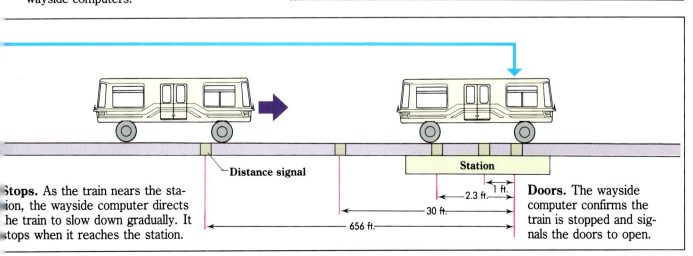

Distance signal

Station

1 ft.
2.3 ft.
30 ft.
656 ft.

Stops. As the train nears the station, the wayside computer directs the train to slow down gradually. It stops when it reaches the station.

Doors. The wayside computer confirms the train is stopped and signals the doors to open.

How Do Subways Get Air?

The air in a subway station would get uncomfortably hot and stuffy if it were not for a system of ventilation ducts and fans *(below)*. Several large air-intake fans bring fresh outside air into the station through a structure that stands at ground level. One fan pumps fresh air into the first basement while an exhaust fan expels stale air to the surface through a second structure. A second intake fan keeps the waiting platform comfortable, and a third supplies fresh air to the tunnel leaving the station. Trains rushing into the station help force stale air out of the tunnel and platform area.

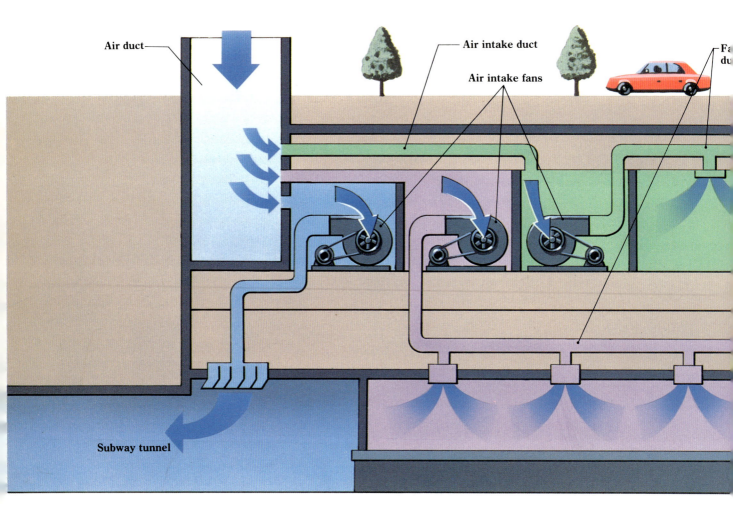

Air duct

Air intake duct

Air intake fans

Subway tunnel

Intake and exhaust fans

Each subway station has an intake ventilator that brings in fresh air from the surface and an exhaust ventilator that expels stale air *(right)*. Air brought into the subway by the intake system passes through a filter to remove dirt before it enters the station. The exhaust duct contains a muffler to dampen the hum generated by the large exhaust fans. Insulation in the exhaust duct reduces vibration, helping to quiet the ventilation system.

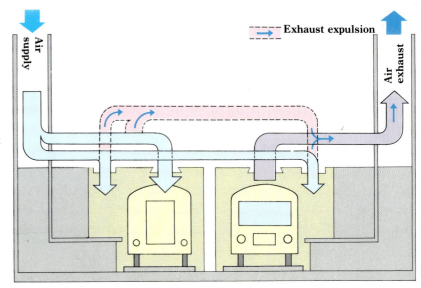

Air supply

Exhaust expulsion

Air exhaust

Air duct structure. This one is disguised as a decorative building.

Muffler system. Walls within the air duct structure quiet fan noise.

Exhaust fans. Several large fans ventilate a subway station.

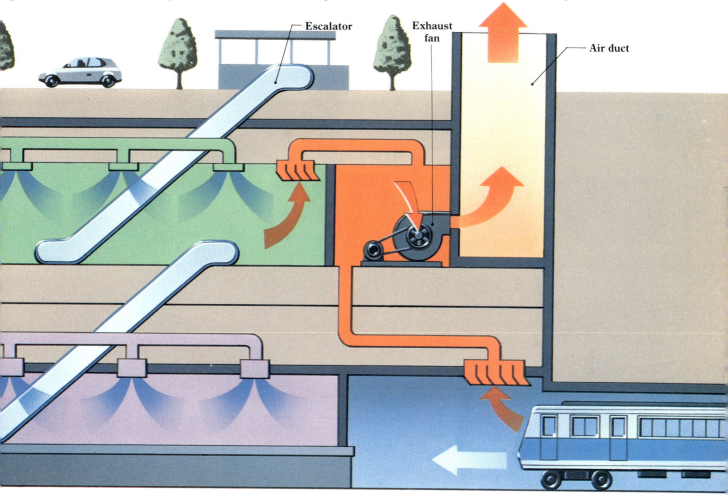

Escalator

Exhaust fan

Air duct

Tunnel ventilation

Subway tunnels between stations also have air intake vents and exhaust ducts to sweep excess heat from the system (*below, left*). The trains force some stale air from the tunnels, and exhaust fans provide the rest of the ventilation (*below, right*). The ducts also create a release for the strong winds that can develop as trains speed through the tunnels.

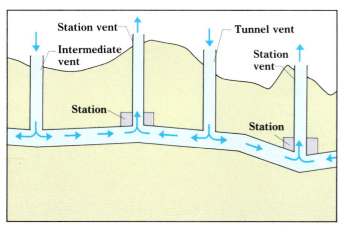

Station vent

Tunnel vent

Intermediate vent

Station vent

Station

Station

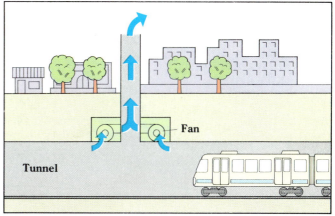

Fan

Tunnel

How Do Monorails Run on One Rail?

Not all trains run on parallel iron rails. Monorail trains, which rest on or hang from a single beam, have been hauling freight and people since 1824. Today, monorails serve as commuter and sightseeing trains in several cities around the world. Rubber wheels guide the monorail along a single concrete beam containing the track and electrical power lines. Some monorails sit on the track, straddling it like a saddlebag *(below)*. Others hang from an overhead beam resembling a giant lamppost. Though monorails require less space than trains that run on two tracks, they are more complicated to build.

Straddle-type monorail

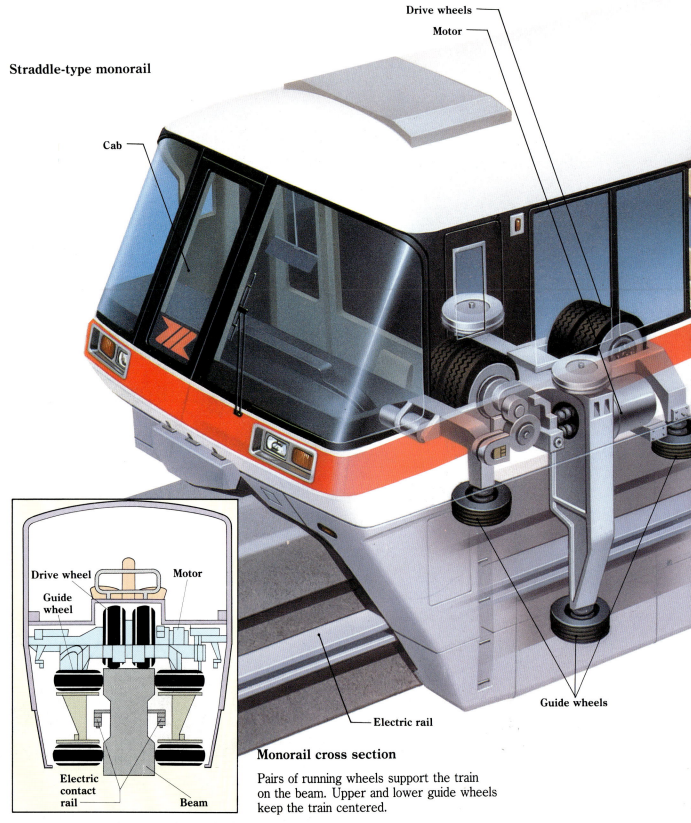

Drive wheels

Motor

Cab

Guide wheels

Electric rail

Drive wheel

Guide wheel

Motor

Electric contact rail

Beam

Monorail cross section

Pairs of running wheels support the train on the beam. Upper and lower guide wheels keep the train centered.

Standard monorail. A straddle-type monorail, with 18 automatic cars, covers 3 miles in Stuttgart, Germany.

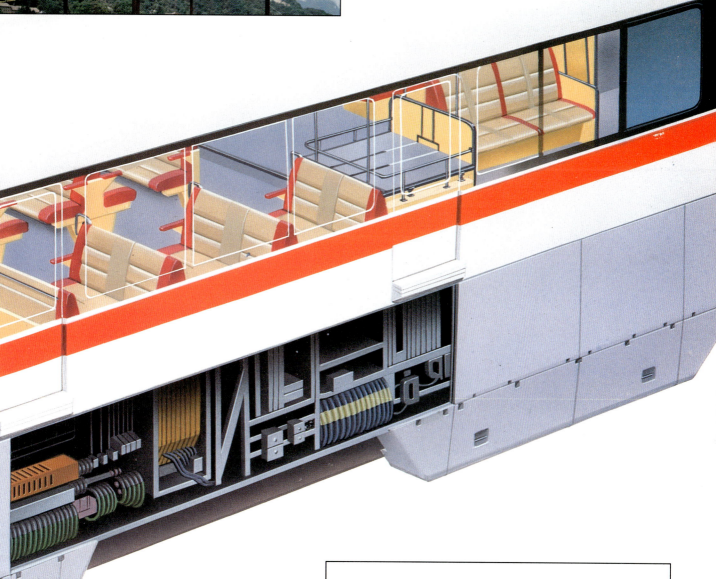

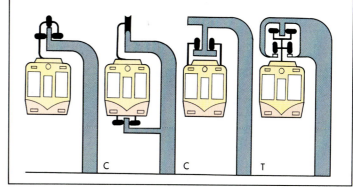

This suspended monorail *(right),* built in 1986, operates year-round in an outdoor zoo in Tampa, Florida.

Suspension monorails

Some monorails hang from overhead supports (different kinds are shown below). The supporting rail provides power to the cars and support for the cars' wheels.

C   C   T

29

What Are Cable Cars?

When hills are too steep for regular trains, cables are used to move cars up and down safely. Modern cable-car systems carry people up and down the sides of mountains and across deep gorges. Some cable cars ride on tracks *(right)*, while others hang from aerial cables. All have some means of grabbing onto a moving cable that runs between two stations. On some cable cars, such as those in San Francisco, a gripman operates a mechanical grip that grasps a cable running underground. To stop the car, the gripman releases the grip. The cable never stops moving.

A cable car pulls commuters up a San Francisco hill.

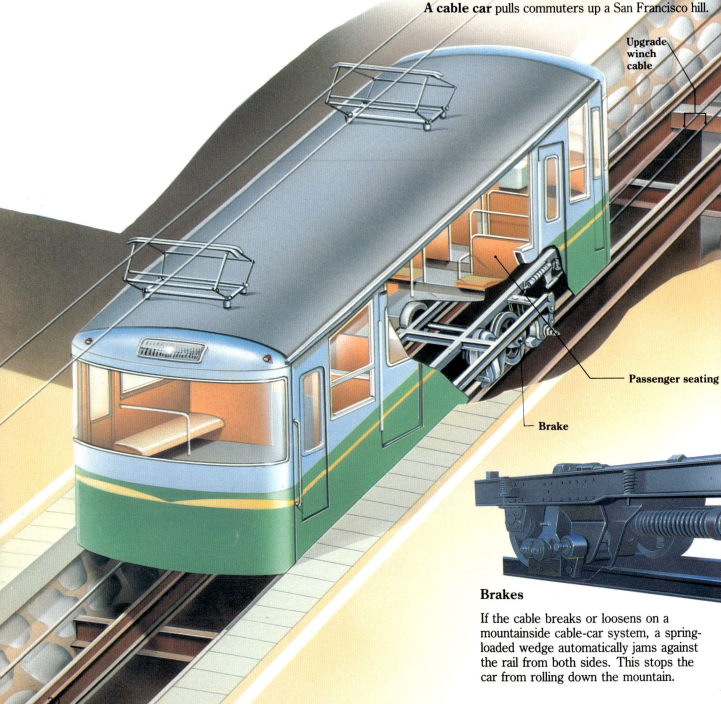

Upgrade winch cable

Passenger seating

Brake

Brakes

If the cable breaks or loosens on a mountainside cable-car system, a spring-loaded wedge automatically jams against the rail from both sides. This stops the car from rolling down the mountain.

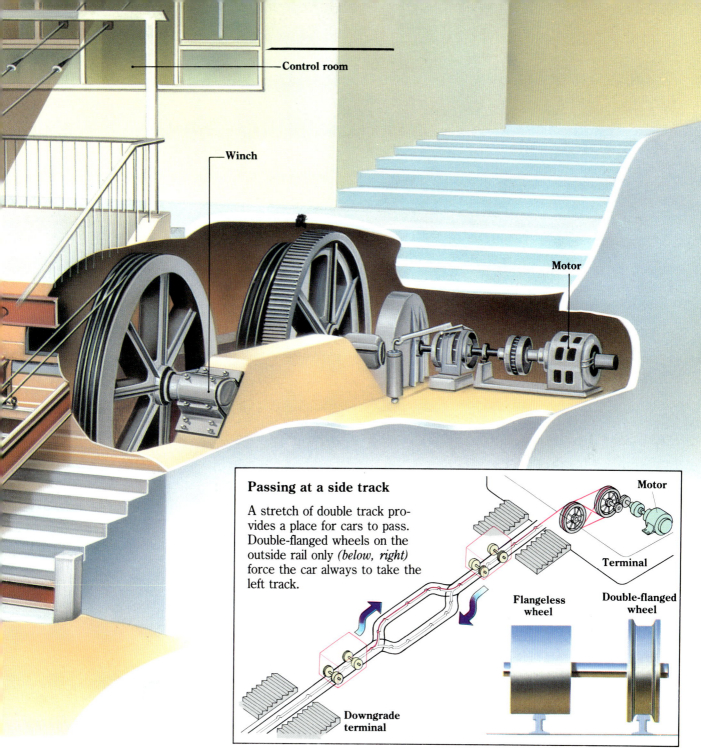

Control room

Winch

Motor

Passing at a side track

A stretch of double track provides a place for cars to pass. Double-flanged wheels on the outside rail only *(below, right)* force the car always to take the left track.

Motor

Terminal

Downgrade terminal

Flangeless wheel

Double-flanged wheel

Ropeway system

In a ropeway, or funicular, system, aerial cable cars move up and down the mountain on two cables. The car's wheels roll over a supporting standing cable *(top left)*. Grabbers latch on to the moving running cable, which pulls the car between stations. Guide rails at each station release the grabbers and remove the cars from the cables. When the car is ready to return, it moves from the guide rail onto the cables. A weight at the downhill station keeps the cables tight.

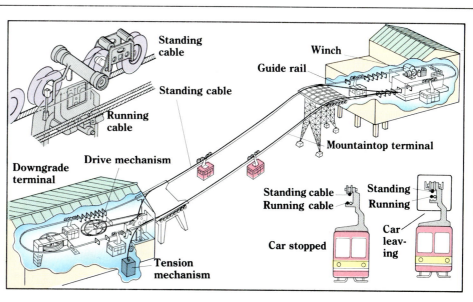

Standing cable

Standing cable

Running cable

Winch

Guide rail

Downgrade terminal

Drive mechanism

Mountaintop terminal

Standing cable
Running cable

Standing
Running

Car stopped

Car leaving

Tension mechanism

How Do Supertrains Run?

To compete with air travel, trains have had to become faster. Today, high-speed trains travel routinely at speeds close to 190 miles per hour. While that's slow compared to a jet's cruising speed, supertrains carry far more passengers and can deliver them right into the heart of a city instead of miles away at an airport. In Japan, high-speed trains carry 300,000 people a day between major cities. Britain, France, and Germany also have popular high-speed train systems.

Supertrains owe their speed to advanced aerodynamic design, high-efficiency electric engines, improved suspension systems, and new techniques for laying track that reduce vibration to a minimum. Long stretches of straightaway and long, banked curves allow the trains to cruise at maximum speed. Computerized automatic train control systems make for safe travel at these high speeds.

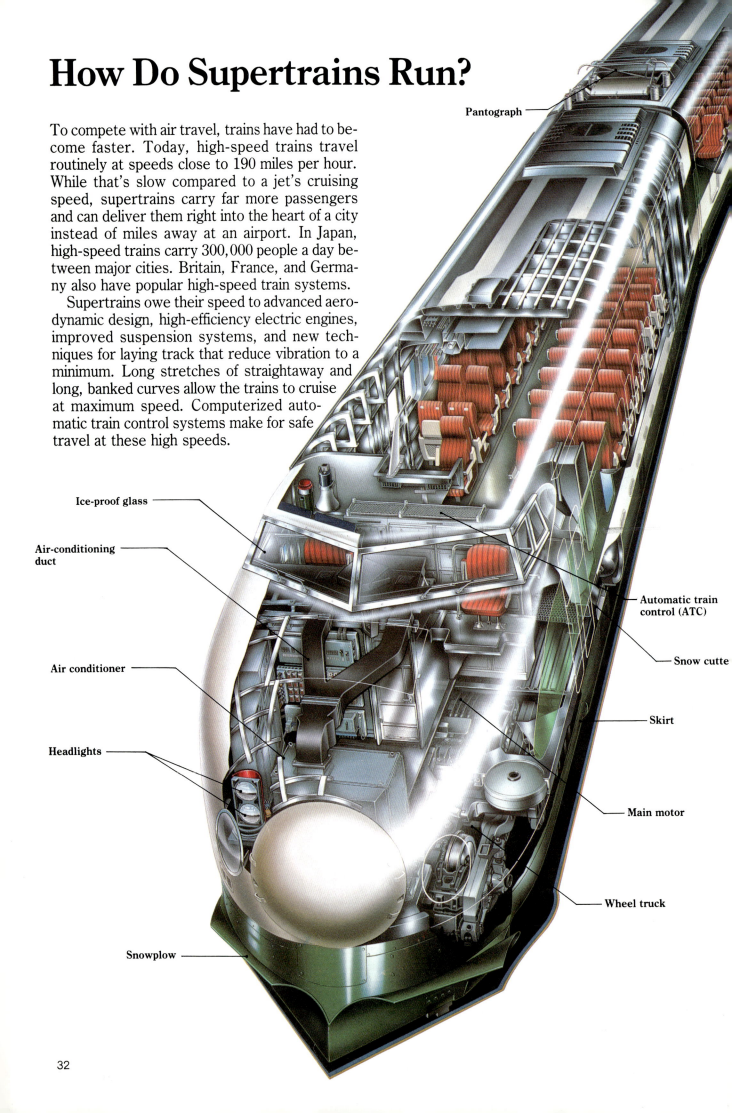

Pantograph

Ice-proof glass

Air-conditioning duct

Air conditioner

Headlights

Snowplow

Automatic train control (ATC)

Snow cutte

Skirt

Main motor

Wheel truck

Wheel truck

The two electric motors on each wheel truck, or bogie, drive the wheels. The disc brakes are lined with heat-resistant alloys. Air-spring suspension gives a smooth ride.

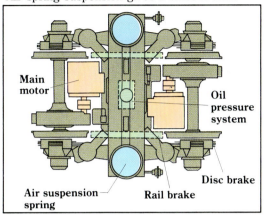

Pantograph

The pantograph gets power through the sink from overhead electric lines. Its small, diamond-shaped framework provides strength and reduces resistance.

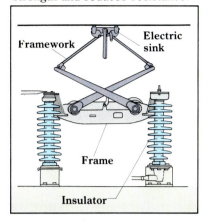

Long rail construction

For a smoother ride, high-speed trains run on rails 1,625 yards long. The joints between rails expand and contract little as the temperature changes.

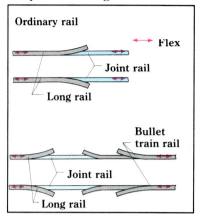

The bullet train

The Japanese bullet trains, or Shinkansen line, formed the first working high-speed train system. When the line opened in 1964, the trains ran from Tokyo to Osaka in just over three hours at an average speed of 100 miles per hour. Now, the Shinkansen line has 263 trains daily, each seating 1,300 passengers, and the journey from Tokyo to Osaka takes two hours and 52 minutes, with a top speed of 136 miles per hour.

Like other high-speed trains, bullet trains are designed with a sloping nose to reduce drag and noise. Windows are shatterproof to withstand sudden changes of pressure as the train enters tunnels. And because of the risk of earthquakes in Japan, the train does not have a heavy locomotive but spreads out its power through a number of power units.

Record-breaking trains

In 1956 a French train set a train speed record of 205 miles per hour. The train's wheels began spinning, and it could go no faster. Experts proclaimed that trains would never top 250 mph. They were proved wrong. In 1988 the German Intercity Express (far right) set a new record of 252 mph, and in 1990 the French Train à Grande Vitesse (near right) hit 320 mph.

France's TGV

Germany's ICE

What Will Future Trains Be Like?

If engineers in Germany, Japan, and the United States succeed, the next generation of trains will not have engines, nor will they travel on rails. In fact, they won't even have wheels, axles, transmissions, motors, or brakes. Instead, they will float, or levitate, on a magnetic cushion just above a rail, and energy-efficient electromagnets will alternately push and pull them along the track much like a surfboard riding a wave.

With no friction to slow them except wind resistance, magnetic levitation trains, or maglevs, will be capable of cruising at speeds of 300 miles per hour or more, and will be able to climb over hills instead of passing through them in tunnels that are expensive to construct. The track's design will make derailments virtually impossible, and with no engines or wheels, maglev trains will be almost silent.

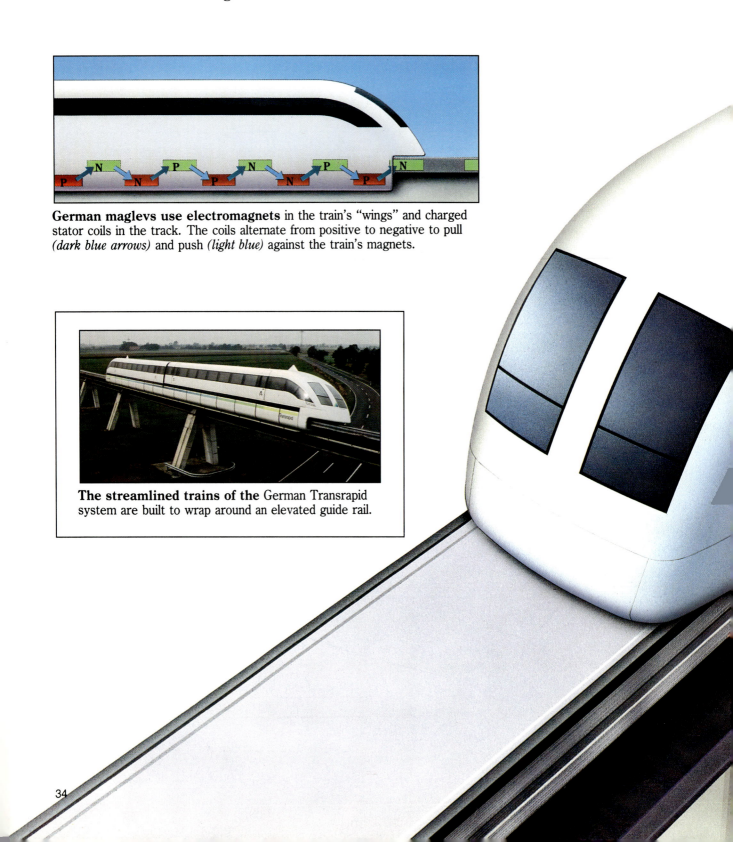

German maglevs use electromagnets in the train's "wings" and charged stator coils in the track. The coils alternate from positive to negative to pull *(dark blue arrows)* and push *(light blue)* against the train's magnets.

The streamlined trains of the German Transrapid system are built to wrap around an elevated guide rail.

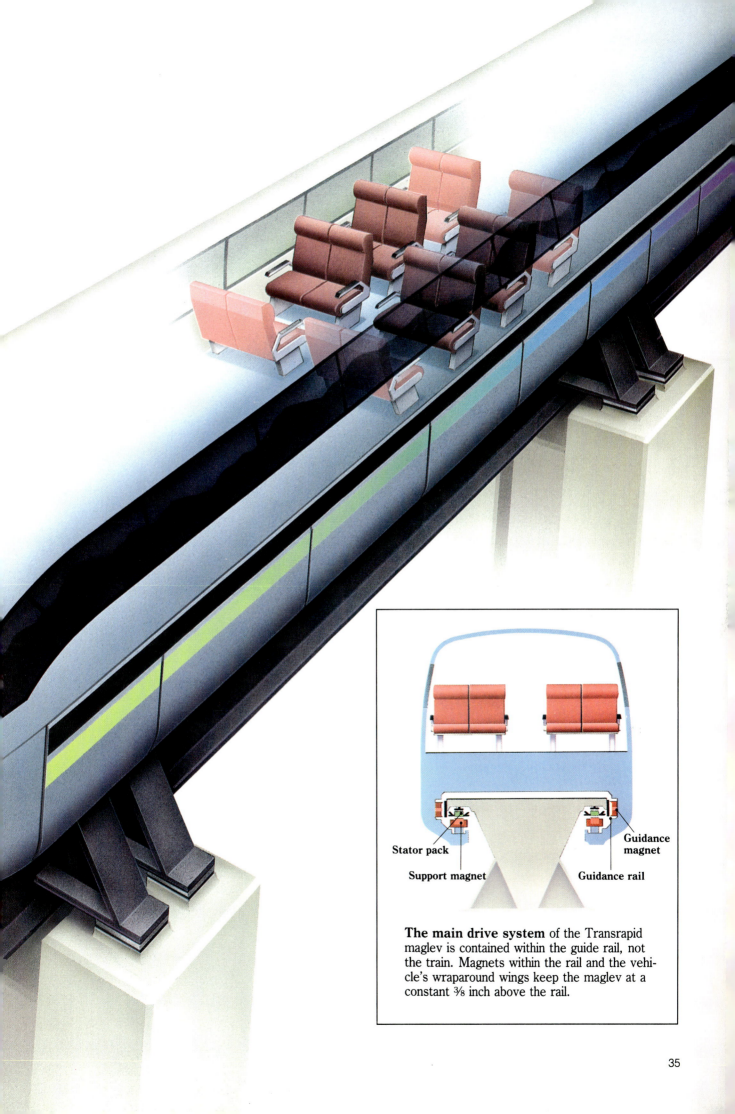

The main drive system of the Transrapid maglev is contained within the guide rail, not the train. Magnets within the rail and the vehicle's wraparound wings keep the maglev at a constant ⅜ inch above the rail.

Stator pack

Support magnet

Guidance magnet

Guidance rail

2
The Machine That Moves Humanity

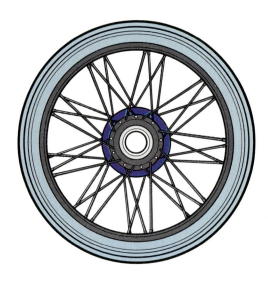

People have been fascinated for centuries with the idea of the automobile—a carriage that moves itself. In fact, that's just what the name automobile means. The first automobile, appearing in 1769, was a steam-powered three-wheeler invented by a Frenchman named Nicolas-Joseph Cugnot. Although Cugnot's machine was rather impractical, it started a chain of events that has profoundly changed the way human beings work, play, and inhabit the world. Today the automobile provides convenient, relatively inexpensive, and enjoyable transportation for people from all walks of life.

Cugnot would scarcely recognize his invention in the automobiles of today, so much has it been changed, redesigned, and improved. Engineers have added computer assistance and called on new materials. New fuels, new aerodynamics, new tire designs, and new technologies have made the automobile—in its many forms—all but indispensable in the lives of millions of people on the planet. This chapter will explore the internal workings of this complex machine and examine the spirit of invention and adventure that has put it on the street in every nation of the world.

Automobile wheels, like the machines they carry, come in a variety of designs, sizes, and materials. Wheel construction contributes greatly to a car's safe and efficient performance.

Who Built the First Automobile?

Early inventors tried to power self-propelled vehicles with wind or a steam jet. But in 1769 French artillery officer Nicolas-Joseph Cugnot built what historians view as the world's first automobile *(below)*. His three-wheeled vehicle got its power from a coal-fired boiler that drove two alternating cylinders, with piston rods anchored to the front wheel *(below, bottom)*. This invention attained nearly 3 mph but was hard to steer, since the tiller had to turn the heavy boiler with the front wheel. This gave Cugnot another place in history. On its first run, his machine knocked down a wall, in the world's first auto accident.

Cugnot's remarkable steam car

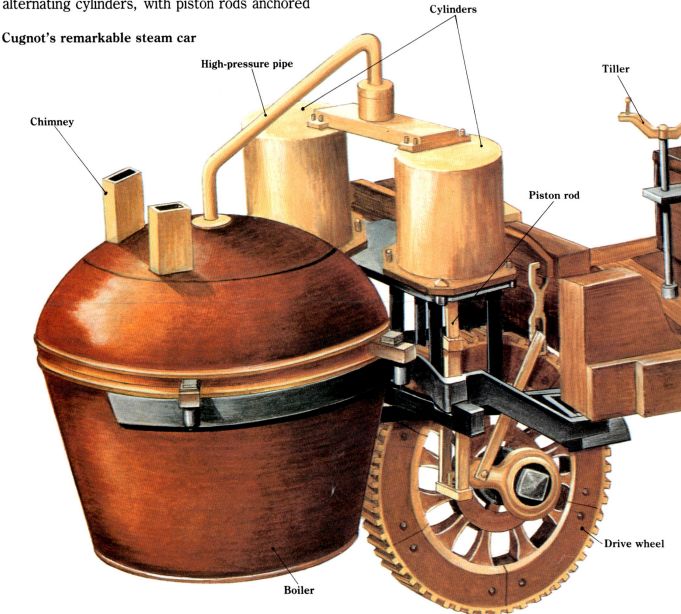

Chimney

High-pressure pipe

Cylinders

Tiller

Piston rod

Boiler

Drive wheel

Driven by high-pressure steam

Steam from the front-mounted boiler passed through high-pressure pipes alternately into the two cylinders, one on each side of the front wheel. In each cylinder, the steam drove the piston rod downward to press on the crank on that side of the wheel *(near right)*. On the upstroke *(far right)*, a ratchet inside the wheel let the wheel spin, while the piston rod pulled the crank upward. A rocking beam linked the two cylinders and kept them working together in alternating rhythm.

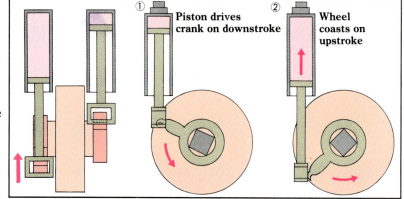

① Piston drives crank on downstroke

② Wheel coasts on upstroke

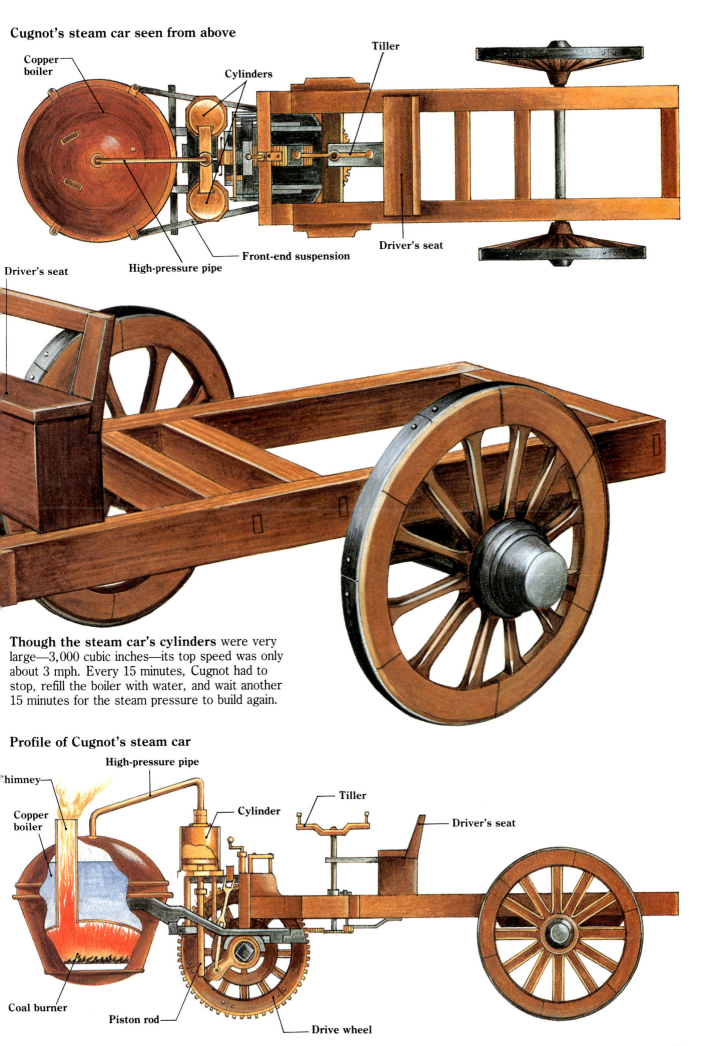

Cugnot's steam car seen from above

Copper boiler

Cylinders

Tiller

Driver's seat

Front-end suspension

High-pressure pipe

Driver's seat

Driver's seat

Though the steam car's cylinders were very large—3,000 cubic inches—its top speed was only about 3 mph. Every 15 minutes, Cugnot had to stop, refill the boiler with water, and wait another 15 minutes for the steam pressure to build again.

Profile of Cugnot's steam car

High-pressure pipe

Chimney

Copper boiler

Cylinder

Tiller

Driver's seat

Coal burner

Piston rod

Drive wheel

Where Does a Car Get Its Power?

A car can be seen as a mechanical device that releases energy from gasoline in order to turn the car's wheels in a controlled way. The gasoline is drawn into each of the engine's cylinders *(below)* in turn. Inside each cylinder, the gasoline burns. The energy that is released from the fuel moves the cylinder's piston. The piston, pushed down in its cylinder like a fist within a sleeve, transfers the energy through the car's crankshaft to the clutch, which controls the transmission.

The transmission gears pass the crankshaft's turning motion to the drive shaft. The spinning drive shaft, attached to the differential gears, not only transfers energy to the drive axles—mounted at right angles to the drive shaft—but also lets the left and right wheels turn at different speeds when necessary, as when the car goes around turns.

Anatomy of a car's power train

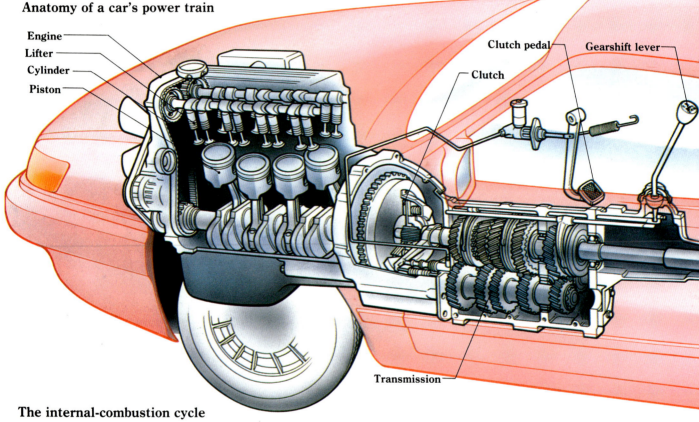

The internal-combustion cycle

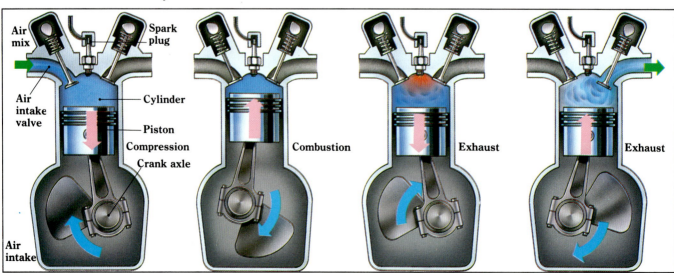

During the intake stroke, the piston moves down, and a mixture of gas and air is drawn into the cylinder. As the piston rises, the mixture is compressed. When the spark plug ignites the mixture, combustion—burning—of the gasoline forces the piston down. When the piston rises again, it forces exhaust gases out past the exhaust valve.

Mixing an explosive gasoline mist

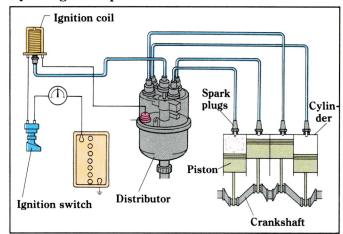

Carburetor

Float

Fuel pump

Cylinder

Piston

Accelerator

Gasoline tank

The accelerator cues the carburetor to mix gasoline with air, producing a mist of fuel. The mist is then drawn into the cylinders, to be ignited by the spark plug.

Sparking the explosion

Ignition coil

Spark plugs

Cylinder

Piston

Ignition switch

Distributor

Crankshaft

The ignition coil converts low voltage from the battery to high voltage. The distributor sends this electricity to the spark plugs, which ignite the fuel mixture in the cylinders.

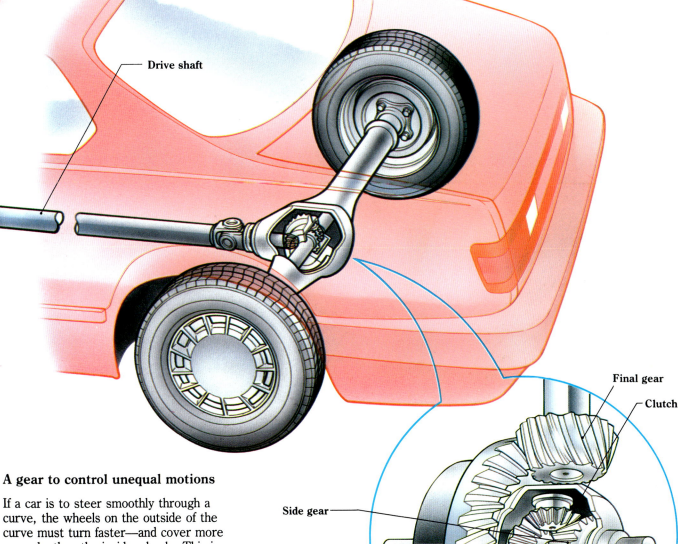

Drive shaft

Final gear

Clutch

Side gear

Ring gear

Pinion gear

Drive-shaft differential gear

A gear to control unequal motions

If a car is to steer smoothly through a curve, the wheels on the outside of the curve must turn faster—and cover more ground—than the inside wheels. This is made possible by the differential. This intricate assembly of gears, cogs, and pinions, connecting the drive shaft to the rear axles, controls the rotation speeds of both axles, even letting them turn at different speeds as necessary.

How Does a Motorcycle Work?

Like an automobile, a motorcycle burns gasoline to produce power and propel itself. The essential difference is that a motorcycle is balanced on two wheels. The engine's power goes to its rear wheel. Although its engine often has far less horsepower, the motorcycle's sleek design and lighter weight let it reach speeds as great as the automobile's. In addition, motorcycles generally accelerate more quickly and are more agile on narrow roads and rough terrain.

Anatomy of a motorcycle

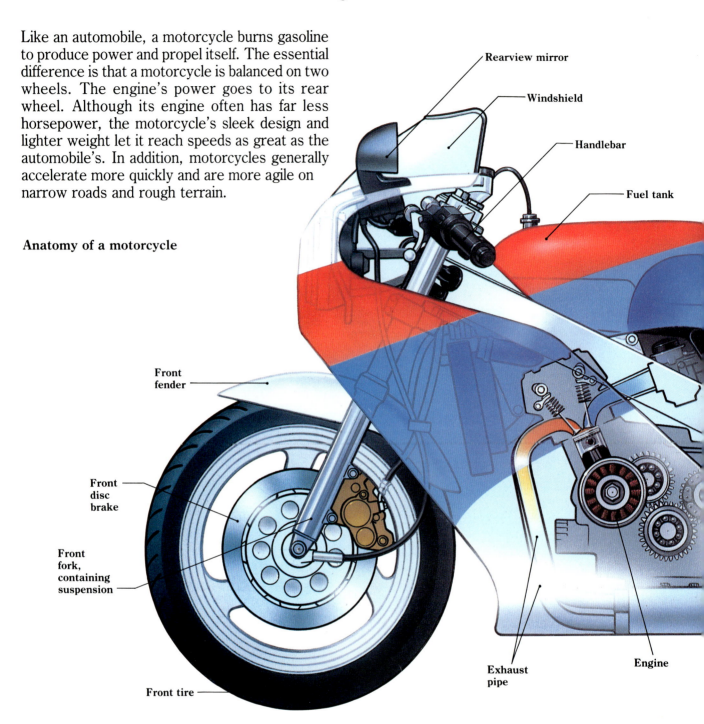

Rearview mirror

Windshield

Handlebar

Fuel tank

Front fender

Front disc brake

Front fork, containing suspension

Front tire

Exhaust pipe

Engine

How the power reaches the wheel

A motorcycle engine operates in much the same way as an automobile engine. Burning fuel in the engine's cylinders pushes the pistons *(far left)*, which turn the crankshaft. The transmission *(left)* transfers the crankshaft's circular motion to the chain that turns the rear wheel. Because the circular motion from the engine is too fast to be sent directly to the rear wheel, it must be slowed down through the gears of the transmission. Ultimately, the rear wheel turns in a ratio of one full rotation for every two crankshaft rotations.

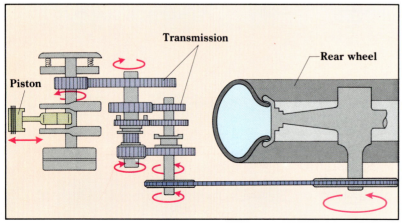

Transmission

Rear wheel

Piston

Light and agile, a motorcycle can reach high speeds.

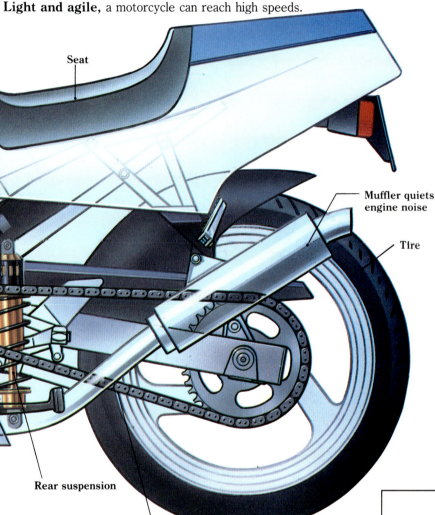

Seat

Muffler quiets
engine noise

Tire

Rear suspension

Chain

Extra power from a two-stroke engine

Four-stroke engines, typically found in automobiles, use a four-part process: air intake, compression, combustion, and exhaust. These steps require two full rotations of the pistons, producing a controlled burn every second time the piston rises. A motorcycle's two-stroke engine *(right)* performs the same processes in each piston circuit—intake and compression as the piston rises *(near right)*, followed by combustion and exhaust *(far right)* on the downstroke. This should make a two-stroke engine twice as powerful as a four-stroke running at the same revolutions per minute (rpm). Engine size and friction do reduce the advantage—but the two-stroke engine is still about 1.5 times as powerful as the four-stroke.

Easing the ride

The motorcycle's spring-loaded suspension system, installed on both wheels, cushions the rider and the engine from the impact of bumps in the road.

Front-wheel suspension

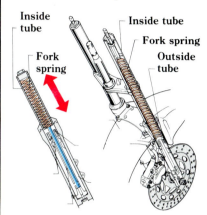

Inside
tube

Fork
spring

Inside tube

Fork spring

Outside
tube

Shock-absorbing springs, encased in hollow forks filled with oil, reduce vibration.

Rear-wheel suspension

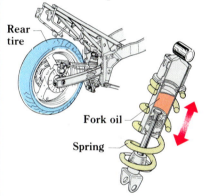

Rear
tire

Fork oil

Spring

The rear shock absorbers are mounted on the frame, one on each side of the wheel.

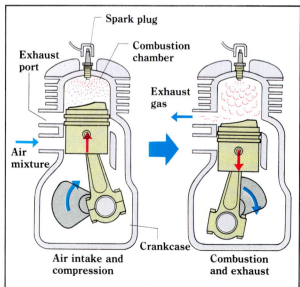

Spark plug

Combustion
chamber

Exhaust
port

Exhaust
gas

Air
mixture

Crankcase

Air intake and
compression

Combustion
and exhaust

How Do Brakes Stop a Car?

The two basic types of brake system—drum brakes and disc brakes—both stop a car by creating friction at its wheels. Drum brakes cause friction by pressing pads against the inside of a drum in the wheel assembly *(opposite, bottom)*. Disc brakes, newer and more popular, simply grip a disc between two pads *(below)*. In both kinds of brake systems, when the driver presses the brake pedal, fluid-filled hoses called brake lines *(below)* carry the pressure to the brakes.

Brake fluid container

Disc brake

Master cylinder

Brake pedal

Putting the squeeze on a disc

The disc brake *(left)* consists of a caliper (1) holding brake pads (2) on both sides of a disc (3) bolted to the wheel. When the driver presses the brake pedal, the caliper pinches the pads against the disc, slowing the wheel. Disc brakes are more reliable than drum brakes for two reasons—they cool more quickly and shed water faster.

The disc brake's calipers straddle the disc *(top right)* and hold the brake pads. Brake-pedal pressure raises the pressure on the brake fluid *(bottom right)*, which presses the pads against the disc.

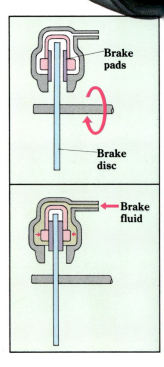

Brake pads

Brake disc

Brake fluid

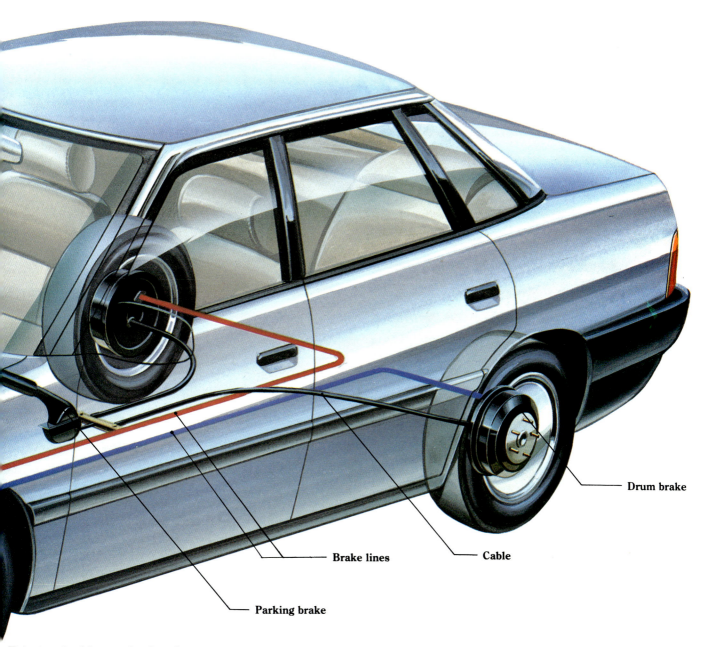

Drum brake

Brake lines

Cable

Parking brake

Friction inside a spinning drum

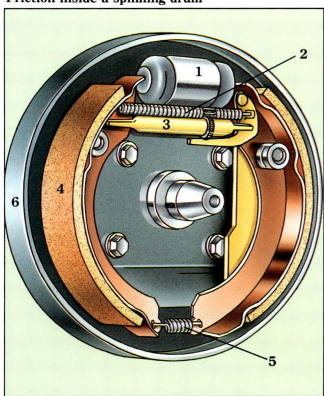

When the brake pedal is pressed, the wheel cylinder (1) presses the brake shoes (4 and its mate) apart, pivoting on the anchor (5). The shoes press against the drum (6), attached to the wheel. When the pedal is released, the return spring (2) moves the shoes to their original positions. The adjuster (3) is used to set the shoes' positions.

At rest, the return spring *(top right)* holds the brake shoes away from the spinning drum. Pressure from the brake line *(bottom right)* moves the pistons in the wheel cylinder, pressing the brake shoes against the drum to slow the wheel with friction.

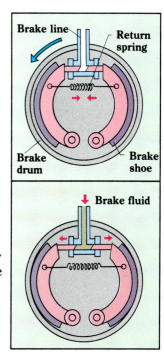

Brake line

Return spring

Brake drum

Brake shoe

Brake fluid

What Does a Transmission Do?

A car's transmission sends turning force—called torque—from the car's engine to its wheels. The transmission's gears also adjust the force so it can be used for different kinds of driving. A car climbing a steep hill must do so in a lower gear than a car cruising on a flat expressway. Lower gears provide more torque, in order to move the car slowly; higher gears provide more speed.

Every transmission is either manual or automatic. To shift gears in a car with a manual transmission *(right)*, a driver first presses the clutch pedal, releasing the engine from the transmission. Next the driver moves the gearshift lever to select another gear and lets the clutch out, reengaging the transmission with the engine, so that power again reaches the wheels. Automatic transmissions measure the position of the gas pedal relative to the speed of the car and shift automatically.

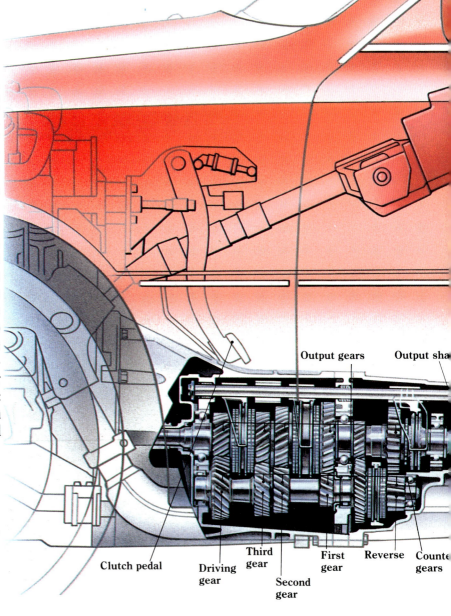

Output gears   Output sha

Clutch pedal   Driving gear   Third gear   Second gear   First gear   Reverse   Counte gears

Manual transmission

These diagrams show how shifting realigns a transmission's gears. For each gear used, engine power takes a different path *(red arrows)* through the gearbox and exerts different force on the wheels.

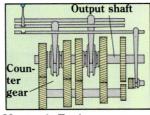

Neutral. Engine energy does not reach the wheels.

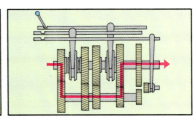

First. The largest gear locks with its mate on the countershaft. Slow but powerful.

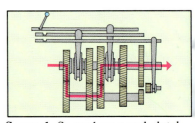

Second. Second gear and clutch gear engage. Top speed is about 15 to 25 mph.

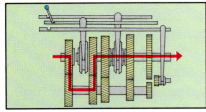

Third. The third gear and the clutch gear engage for higher speed at a lower torque.

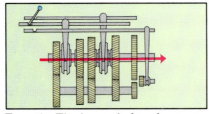

Fourth. The input shaft and output shaft engage for very low torque and maximum speed.

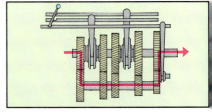

Reverse. The reverse gear engages the countershaft and main gears to turn the output shaft in reverse.

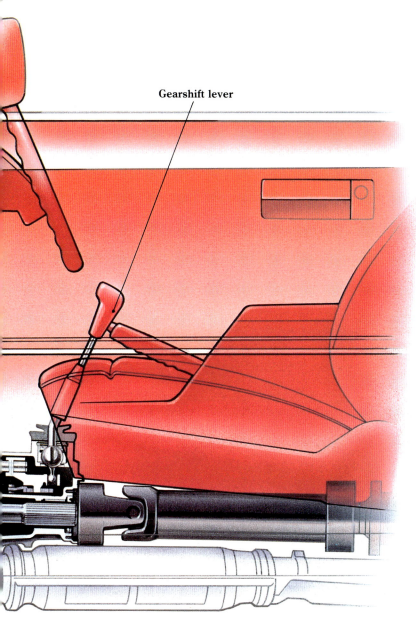

Gearshift lever

How an engine's accelerator works

An engine's revolutions per minute (rpm) are determined by the amount of fuel passing through the carburetor into the cylinders. This flow of fuel is regulated by the carburetor's throttle plate, which is in turn controlled by a pedal called the accelerator, on the floor in front of the driver.

The driver's foot pressure on the accelerator opens the throttle plate and increases the flow of fuel. When the driver releases the pressure on the accelerator, the throttle plate closes and the amount of fuel is reduced. This decreases both the engine's rpm and the automobile's speed.

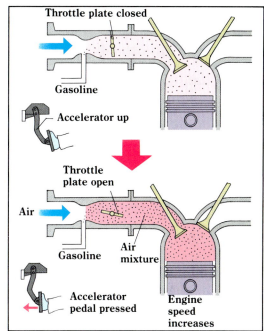

Throttle plate closed

Gasoline

Accelerator up

Throttle plate open

Air

Gasoline

Air mixture

Accelerator pedal pressed

Engine speed increases

Automatic transmission

An automatic transmission has no clutch pedal for the driver to use. Instead, the torque converter and planetary gear *(right)* work together to disengage the engine from the drive shaft when a shift in gears is needed, and reengage it after the shift is made. Once the driver sets the gear lever for driving, the transmission automatically selects the gear, adjusting to the car's performance.

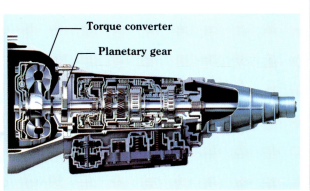

Torque converter

Planetary gear

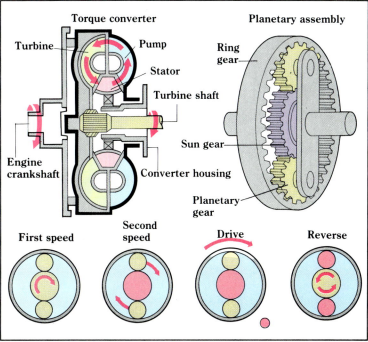

Torque converter

Turbine

Pump

Stator

Turbine shaft

Engine crankshaft

Converter housing

Planetary assembly

Ring gear

Sun gear

Planetary gear

First speed

Second speed

Drive

Reverse

What Is Four-Wheel Drive?

Most cars are built with two-wheel drive (2WD), which sends the engine's power to only one pair of wheels—either the front two or the rear two. Four-wheel drive (4WD) is a specialized drive system that can route the power from the engine to all four of the car's wheels. It does this through additional couplings and differential gears, as shown at right.

In the earliest vehicles equipped with 4WD, the driver decided when to use the 4WD. Now, however, some cars come with full-time 4WD, which engages automatically in response to certain driving conditions.

Two-wheel drive *(right)* transfers the engine's power *(pink)* to two wheels—here, the rear wheels—while four-wheel drive *(far right)* powers all four wheels.

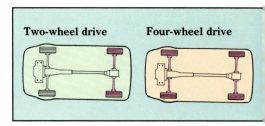

Two-wheel drive   Four-wheel drive

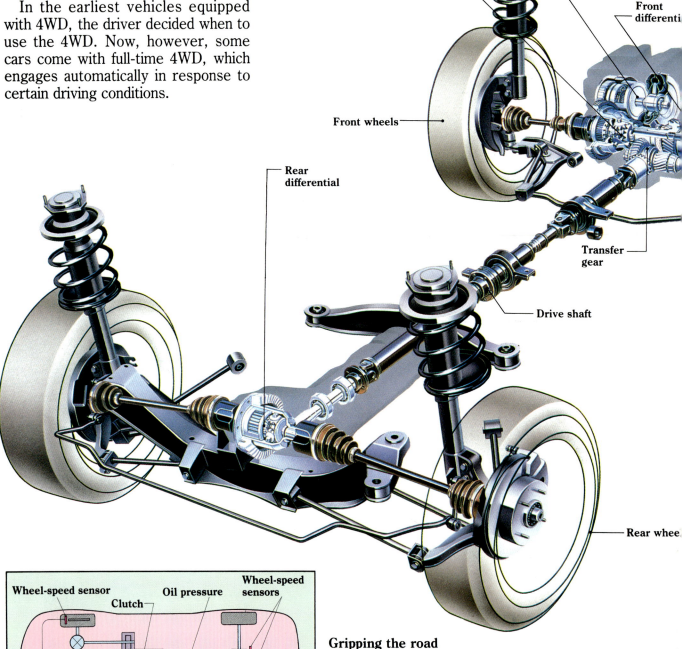

Center differential

Automatic transmission

Front differenti

Front wheels

Rear differential

Transfer gear

Drive shaft

Rear whee

Wheel-speed sensor

Clutch

Oil pressure

Wheel-speed sensors

G-sensor

Wheel-speed sensor   Computer

Gripping the road

On slippery or uneven surfaces, 4WD helps a car move safely. Sensors monitor the speeds of all four wheels. If any wheel starts to spin, the computer takes power away from the sensor of that wheel and redistributes it among the wheels that have a better grip on the road.

Four wheels at four speeds

The center differential controls the individual turning speed of all four wheels. In fact, it allows each wheel to turn at a different speed if necessary—as when the car goes around a turn. Another complex gear called the viscous coupling makes the 4WD system fully automatic, and therefore safer.

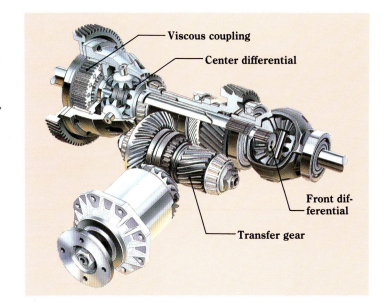

Viscous coupling

Center differential

Front differential

Transfer gear

Inside the viscous coupling

The viscous coupling, about 4 inches long, is occupied by a disk-shaped plate and filled with thick, syrupy silicon fluid. Inner shafts accept power from the engine. Outer plates, connected to the drive shaft, then transfer the power to the rear wheels.

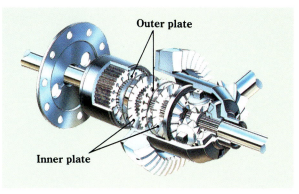

Outer plate

Inner plate

How the viscous coupling works

If the wheels do not slip, both the inner and outer plates will turn at the same speed. When a wheel does spin, however, the increased speed of the plate activates the viscous coupling. The coupling then floods the plates with its thick, syrupy fluid to slow wheel rotation. As a result, the wheel stops slipping and steady handling is quickly restored. At the same time, a slowly rotating outer plate, pulled by the rapidly rotating inner plate, increases engine speed. Thus the car avoids skidding without significantly lowering its speed or driving power.

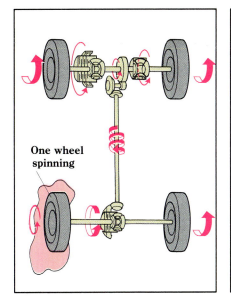

One wheel spinning

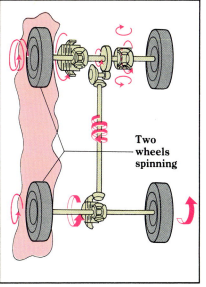

Two wheels spinning

What is optional four-wheel drive?

In vehicles with an optional 4WD system, the driver uses a special clutch *(pink handle)* to change between 2WD and 4WD. When the car is running in 2WD *(right)*, the transfer gear and the dog clutch are disengaged, so that power goes only to the rear wheels. In 4WD *(far right)*, the transfer gear and dog clutch are engaged, and power is transferred by a second drive shaft to the car's front wheels.

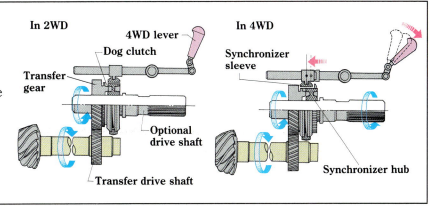

In 2WD

4WD lever

Dog clutch

Transfer gear

Optional drive shaft

Transfer drive shaft

In 4WD

Synchronizer sleeve

Synchronizer hub

What Is Four-Wheel Steering?

To steer an ordinary car, the driver turns the steering wheel, changing the direction of the front wheels, while the rear wheels remain aimed straight ahead. This standard system is called two-wheel steering and is abbreviated 2WS. Some manufacturers, however, are building cars with four-wheel steering (4WS).

Although 4WS systems differ, in most of them the rear wheels go in the same direction as the front wheels during turns made at highway speeds. At low speeds, four-wheel steering turns the rear wheels in the opposite direction from that of the front wheels *(opposite, top);* this permits sharper turns that are helpful in city traffic or in tight parking spaces. Most road tests of 4WS systems indicate that they make cars somewhat safer to drive. Four-wheel steering is not yet widely popular, however, because for many drivers, the cost of a 4WS system outweighs the improved performance.

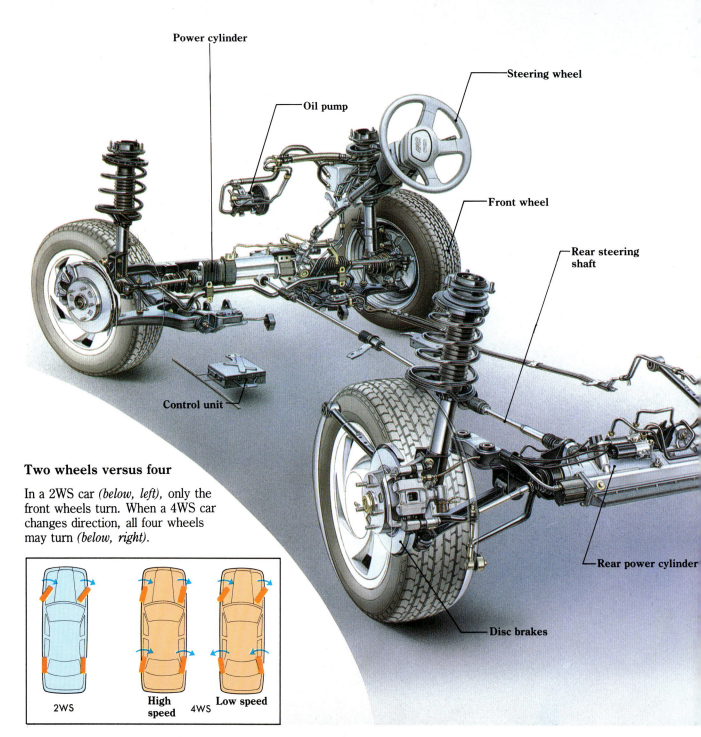

Power cylinder

Oil pump

Steering wheel

Front wheel

Rear steering shaft

Control unit

Rear power cylinder

Disc brakes

Two wheels versus four

In a 2WS car *(below, left),* only the front wheels turn. When a 4WS car changes direction, all four wheels may turn *(below, right).*

2WS

High speed

4WS

Low speed

How 4WS turns wheels

Starting from the same place *(green, below)*, a 2WS car *(blue)* and a 4WS car *(yellow)* make tight, slow turns. Turning the rear wheels gives the 4WS car a smaller turning radius—lets it turn in less space—than the car with 2WS. On a wide turn *(right)*, a 4WS car's tires all aim one way and grip the road better.

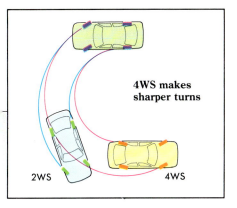

4WS makes sharper turns

2WS   4WS

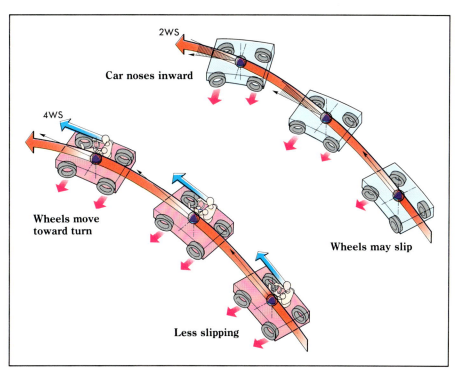

2WS

Car noses inward

4WS

Wheels move toward turn

Less slipping

Wheels may slip

Changing lanes

When changing lanes on a highway, a 2WS car *(far right)* tends to fishtail—its rear end swings out—because its rear wheels aim straight ahead. To correct this motion, the driver has to turn the steering wheel twice before and twice after changing lanes. The 4WS car *(near right)* does not fishtail.

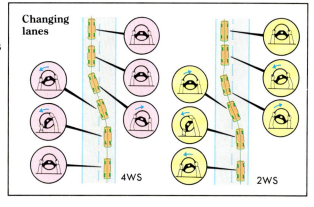

Changing lanes

4WS

2WS

The steering wheel and 4WS

Sensors in a 4WS system monitor how far the driver turns the steering wheel—and thus the front wheels *(right, red line)*—for each curve. For small steering-wheel movements *(first two columns)*, 4WS leaves the rear wheels *(blue line)* straight or turns them the same way as the front wheels. For sharp turns—when the steering wheel turns more than a full turn *(far right)*—4WS turns the rear wheels the opposite way *(below)*.

Rear wheel

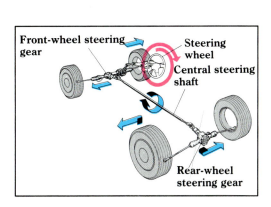

Front-wheel steering gear

Steering wheel

Central steering shaft

Rear-wheel steering gear

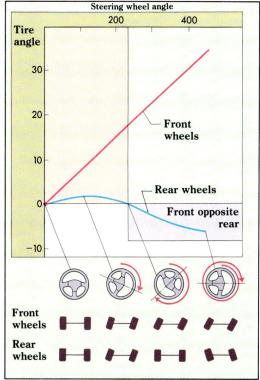

Steering wheel angle

200   400

Tire angle

30

20

10

0

-10

Front wheels

Rear wheels

Front opposite rear

Front wheels

Rear wheels

How Does a Car's Air Bag Work?

In a head-on crash, a car's driver and passengers are thrown forward and can be seriously hurt when they hit the steering wheel, dashboard, or windshield. Air bags protect people during a collision by popping out of the steering wheel or dash and instantly inflating with nitrogen gas.

An air-bag system consists of electronic sensors, an inflater to produce the nitrogen gas, and the bag itself. The sensors are set to ignore collisions at speeds under 10 to 14 mph. In a crash, the bag is fully inflated 1/20 of a second after impact. Then, so the people can escape from the car, the bag collapses after absorbing the initial shock. Air bags can save lives but only in head-on crashes. They are not a substitute for seat belts and shoulder straps.

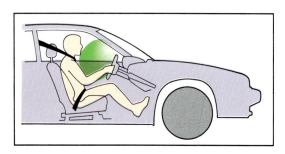

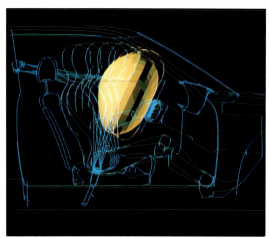

Instant pillow. In a head-on collision, sensors signal the nitrogen-gas inflater. As the bag inflates, it breaks out of its storage place in the steering wheel, becoming a pillow just as the driver is thrown forward.

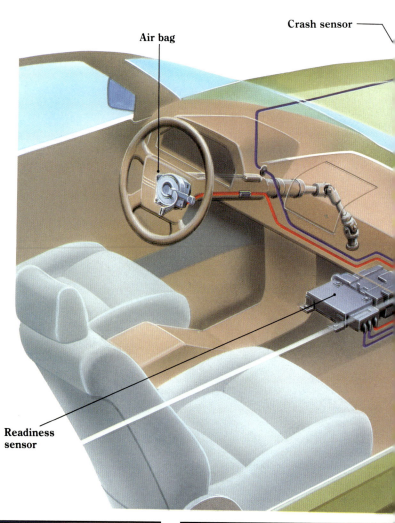

Air bag

Crash sensor

Readiness sensor

An experimental crash at 10 mph

Upon the crash sensors' signals, a heat generator ignites chemicals to produce the nitrogen gas that quickly inflates the air bag.

The fully inflated air bag absorbs the initial impact of the driver's body as it is thrown forward.

Once the driver's body has been cushioned, the bag collapses, softening the shock. Two holes in the back of the bag release the gas.

Sensing a sudden stop

The system's three sensors respond in .01 second to the halting of forward movement at a speed over 10 mph. In each sensor *(below, left)* a roller is poised next to a switch. In a crash *(below, right)*, the roller's momentum rolls it forward over the switch, triggering inflation of the bag.

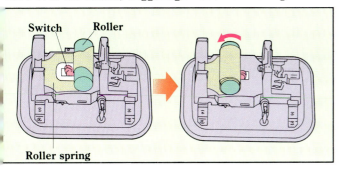

Switch Roller

Roller spring

Crash sensor

Making gas to fill the bag

When signaled by the crash sensors, the inflater *(below)* ignites chemicals that produce nitrogen gas. The gas goes through a filter on its way into the air bag.

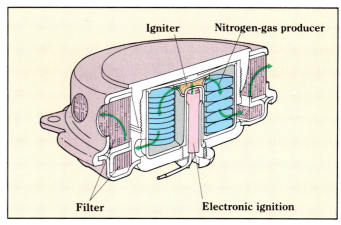

Igniter Nitrogen-gas producer

Filter Electronic ignition

Filling the bag in a split second

As the newly generated nitrogen gas rushes into the air bag, the bag breaks out *(below, middle)* of its compartment in the steering wheel. The bag holds 16 gallons of gas and is inflated within .05 second of impact—less time than it takes for the driver to be thrown toward the windshield.

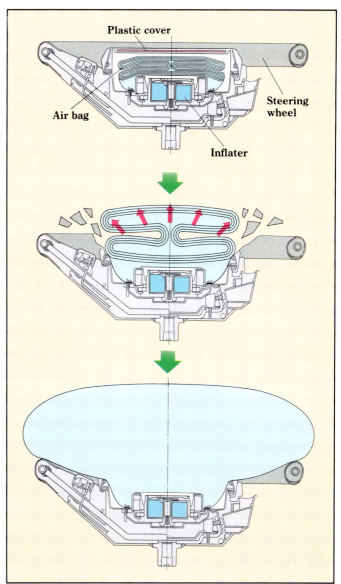

Plastic cover

Air bag

Steering wheel

Inflater

Dual protection. Since the passenger sitting next to the driver is also at risk in an accident, some cars have air bags on both sides. The passenger side is roomier, so the air bag there is usually bigger than the driver's.

What Is a Turbocharged Engine?

To produce the energy that moves the car, an automobile's engine burns a mixture of fuel and air. The more air is added to the mixture, the more horsepower the engine produces. An ordinary engine pulls air into each of its cylinders when the piston pulls down into that cylinder. But a high-performance engine pumps extra air into the cylinders with a device that is called a turbocharger.

A turbocharger contains a turbine driven by the engine's own hot exhaust. The turbocharger's compressor gathers in air, greatly increases its pressure, and then forces the air into the cylinders, where it produces more complete combustion, or burning, of the fuel. By forcing extra air into the cylinders, the turbocharger increases an engine's horsepower without changing the size of the engine itself.

The turbocharger

In an engine turbocharger, the compressor *(blue disk)* takes in fresh air *(blue arrows)* and pushes it at high pressure into the cylinders. The compressor is driven by a turbine *(red disk)*, which gives the turbocharger its name and is turned by hot engine exhaust gases *(red arrows)*. A central bearing supports the compressor and turbine.

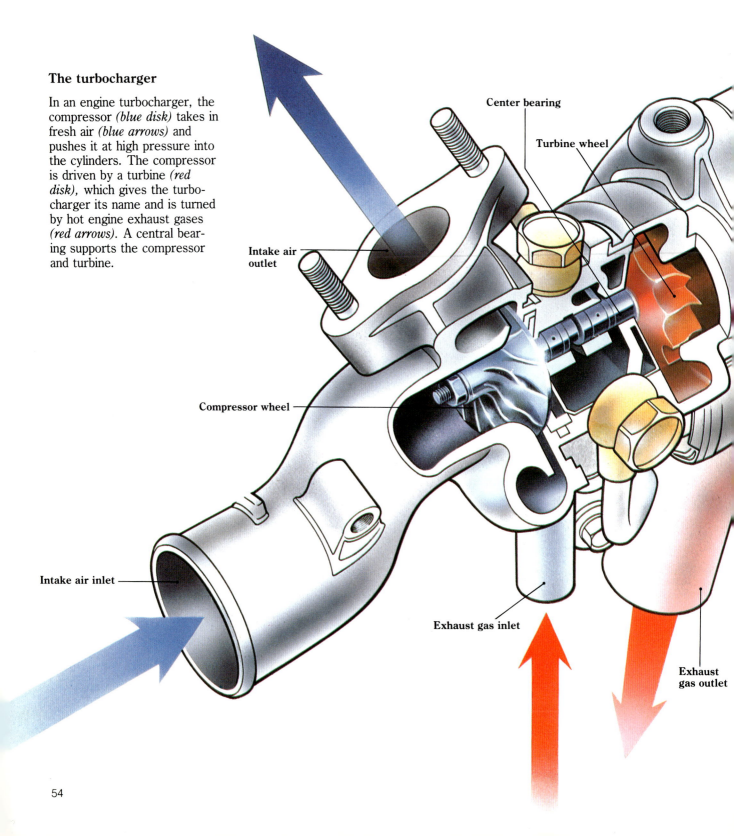

Intake air outlet

Center bearing

Turbine wheel

Compressor wheel

Intake air inlet

Exhaust gas inlet

Exhaust gas outlet

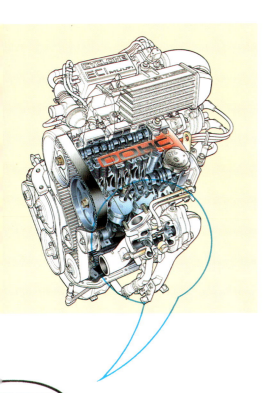

Powerful addition. Mounted on a car engine *(left)*, a turbocharger *(in blue circle)* can boost horsepower. Early turbocharged engines were troubled with a tendency to overheat, but improved models are built into a full range of cars, from high-performance sports cars to compacts.

More horsepower

A turbocharged engine *(below)* uses hot exhaust gases *(pink)* to drive a turbine and force high-pressure air *(blue)* into the cylinders. The release valve vents excess air pressure. This engine's turbocharger *(within blue circle)* is enlarged in the middle drawing, below.

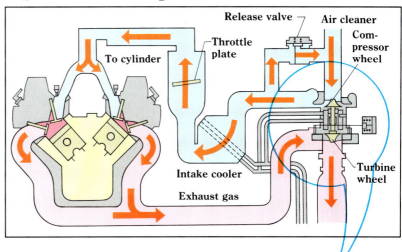

Driven by hot exhaust

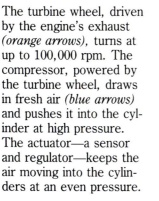

The turbine wheel, driven by the engine's exhaust *(orange arrows),* turns at up to 100,000 rpm. The compressor, powered by the turbine wheel, draws in fresh air *(blue arrows)* and pushes it into the cylinder at high pressure. The actuator—a sensor and regulator—keeps the air moving into the cylinders at an even pressure.

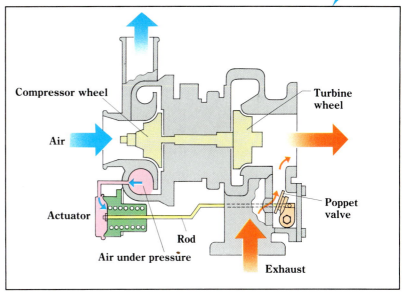

High-pressure intake

Exhaust gases *(orange)* entering the turbine *(far right)* turn the turbine wheel, which drives the compressor wheel that is attached to the same axle. The compressor's spinning fan pulls in fresh air *(blue)* and compresses it, forcing air at high pressure into the cylinders.

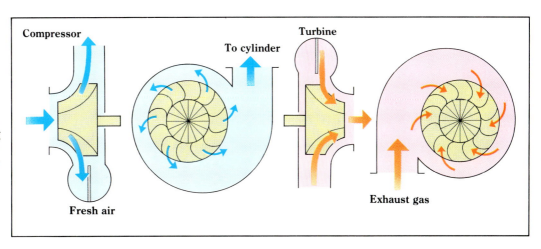

Why Do Tires Have Tread?

If all roads were smooth, dry, and straight, there would be no need for the grooves, or tread, on a tire's surface. Treadless tires, which have greater contact with the road and therefore better traction, would outperform treaded tires on dry pavement. But roads are never perfect. On wet roads, a dangerous layer of water can build up between the road surface and a treadless tire, causing skids and accidents. Treaded tires drain the water safely away and make the tire more stable on rough or curving roads. To keep cars moving safely under a variety of conditions, treaded tires are best.

Cross section of tire
Tread

Reinforcing belts

Tire body

Bead wire hugs wheel rim

Inner layer

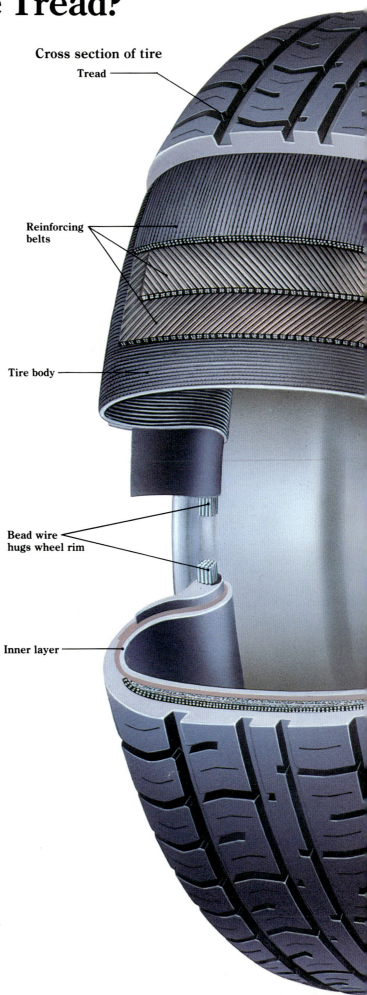

Smooth tires are dangerous tires

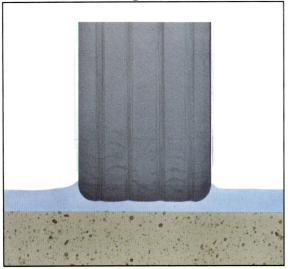

On wet roads, a tire with little or no tread pushes water ahead of it and may begin to float on a layer of water between the tire and the road. This dangerous condition is called hydroplaning.

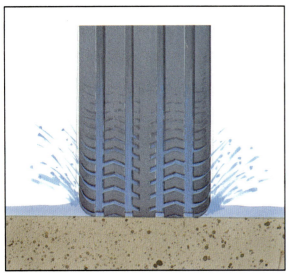

A tire with tread drains water away in its grooves and stays in touch with the road, reducing the risk of skids from hydroplaning.

Wheel

Special tires for special uses

A car's tires are designed to grip the road surface while supporting the car's weight and also to stabilize the ride and help steering. Different driving conditions, however—and different vehicles—call for a wide variety of tire designs.

Bias tires give family cars a smooth ride.

Radial tires provide stability at high speeds.

Studded tires give traction on icy roads.

Rugged tires for 4WD cars endure rough ground.

The rally tire grips most road surfaces.

Bus and truck tires survive long-distance driving.

Dump trucks have large, wide tires.

A tractor tire's oversize tread is ideal for the field.

A lawn mower's wide tires don't cut up grass.

Tires for driving on snow

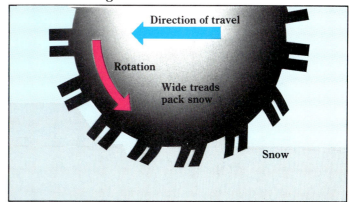

Direction of travel

Rotation

Wide treads pack snow

Snow

Some tires are made of a special rubber that stays flexible in the cold. Under the car's weight, the tires' large, boxy treads pack the snow, forming a hard surface for more traction.

What Makes a Racing Car Different?

A Formula One racing car—named for the special-formula fuel it burns—has a much more powerful engine than a passenger car. The increased power comes from the engine's greater capacity—that is, the total volume of the combustion chambers in its cylinders. In the average passenger car, engine capacity may be 61 cubic inches or less. Formula One racing cars can have three times that capacity, and develop 500 horsepower—four or five times the horsepower of an ordinary car.

To make that additional horsepower most effective, the racing car's body is aerodynamically designed to minimize air resistance. Racing tires are extrawide for secure road contact and traction. Special racing suspension adds stability, helping the car grip the road firmly even as it speeds through tight turns.

A Formula One racing car

In the cockpit, a racing driver follows the car's performance by glancing at an array of gauges showing fuel level, water temperature, oil pressure, and other information.

Heavy-duty carbon-fiber disc brakes *(below)* must survive the heat of high-speed racing.

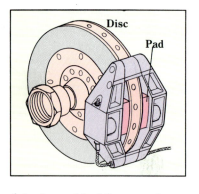

Disc

Pad

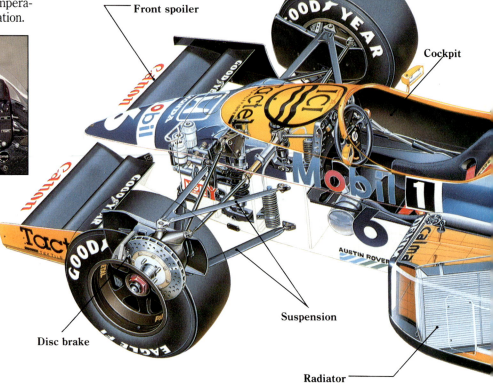

Front spoiler

Cockpit

Suspension

Disc brake

Radiator

A body molded for speed

The low, wide body of a racing car, made of lightweight but strong carbon fiber, is designed to make use of the airflow the car creates at high speeds. The sloped front end *(below, left)* and rear spoilers make the air press down on the car and keep it from becoming airborne.

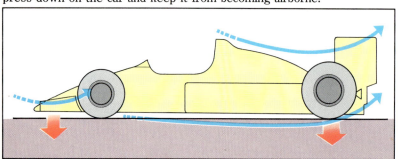

Tires to match track conditions

Wider than those used on ordinary cars, racing tires may have little tread—for dry tracks—or have special tread for rain.

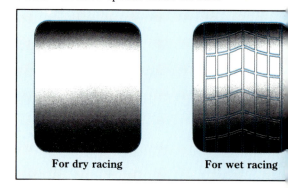

For dry racing

For wet racing

A powerful, high-technology engine

For both power and efficiency, a racing car's engine *(below)* has computerized fuel injection and electronic regulators to control engine rpm, oil and water temperatures, and other vital functions.

Ten cylinders power this special racing engine.

A Formula One racing car *(above)* runs far hotter than a passenger car. Like a passenger car, it throws off excess heat through its radiator, which is cooled by the flow of air *(below)* as the car hurtles around the track at speeds of up to 180 mph.

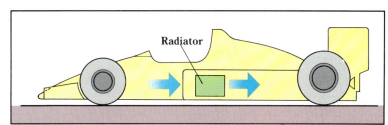

Radiator

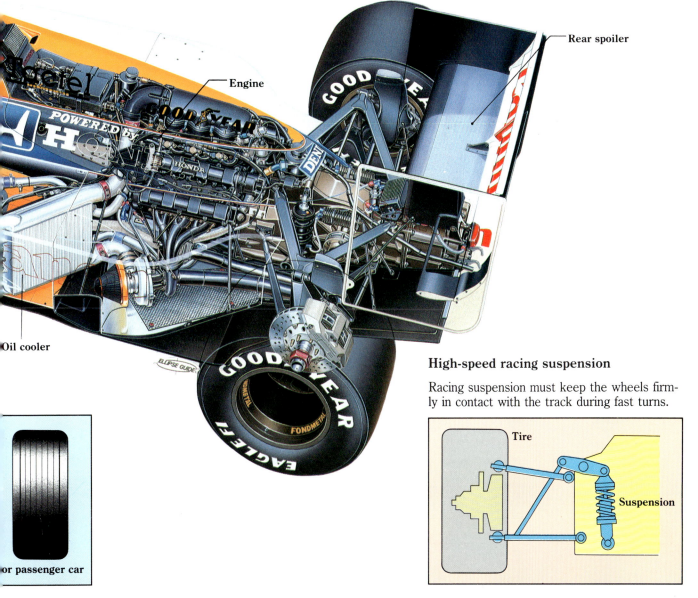

Engine

Rear spoiler

Oil cooler

or passenger car

High-speed racing suspension

Racing suspension must keep the wheels firmly in contact with the track during fast turns.

Tire

Suspension

Can Any Car Drive Itself?

This exotic-looking car, an experimental Mitsubishi Model MSRII, is a highly automated car. Equipped with closed-circuit television and infrared cameras, the car can recognize and react to centerlines and road signs. Using these cameras and its ultrasonic wave sensors—much like a bat's sonar—the car can also detect traffic and other obstacles and adjust the car's speed and direction accordingly.

Even with its futuristic systems and remarkable abilities, this car does not do all the driving. Still, many experts predict that researchers and engineers will someday produce a car that can compensate for its driver's delays in reaction time and errors of judgment.

Information and navigation

In addition to monitoring road and traffic conditions, the navigation system also provides maps and advises the driver on the best routes to take.

Automatic traffic tracking

Sensors track the lead car's LED.

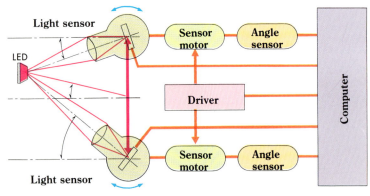

Finding and analyzing the light from the light-emitting diode (LED) on the car ahead, the following car's computer (*right*) makes appropriate speed and steering adjustments to maintain safe distance.

Specialized sensors near the headlights pick up light from an LED on the car ahead.

60

Improving on the driver's eyesight

Between the driver's and passenger's seats are television and infrared cameras that scan the car's surroundings. They then send images to be processed by the car's on-board computer. This system sees and reacts to things that the driver may sometimes overlook, such as oncoming traffic, sudden stops, sharp turns, and hazardous surface conditions. Rather than relaying information to the driver, it simply adjusts the car's speed and direction. As a result, the driver is able to proceed down the road more securely.

The brains of the automated car

This automated car could not function without computers. The on-board computer system co-ordinates data gathered by the car's built-in sensors, cameras, and mechanical devices, processes it with several separate small computers, and sends appropriate signals to the car's various control systems.

A high-speed body

For high-speed driving, this car is equipped with front spoiler, canard, and flaps that adjust automatically, to offer the least air resistance.

Trouble-free parking

In a parking area that has magnetic cables embedded in its surface, the car's automatic parking system senses the magnetic fields of the cables. The car's four magnetic sensors pass data to a computer that tells the wheels which way to turn. Other sensors detect objects so that the car can park without hitting anything.

Canard

Flaps

Front spoiler

Venturi flap

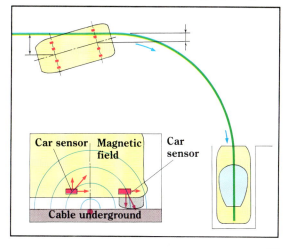

Car sensor | Magnetic field | Car sensor

Cable underground

How Does a Solar-Powered Car Work?

Solar-powered automobiles are still in the experimental stage, and they vary greatly in design, construction, and performance. But all of them, like the cars on these pages, have certain basic similarities. All have solar collecting panels, which absorb sunlight and convert it to electricity. Most store this electricity in special batteries and then use it to power an electric motor that turns the wheels.

Solar cars are designed to make efficient use of their supplies of energy. Most are made of very lightweight materials and shaped to offer minimum wind resistance. Theoretically, a solar car can operate indefinitely, needs no fuel other than sunlight, and produces no pollution. Its disadvantage is that it cannot work at night or on overcast days. Researchers are working to overcome these limitations.

The *Southern Cross*

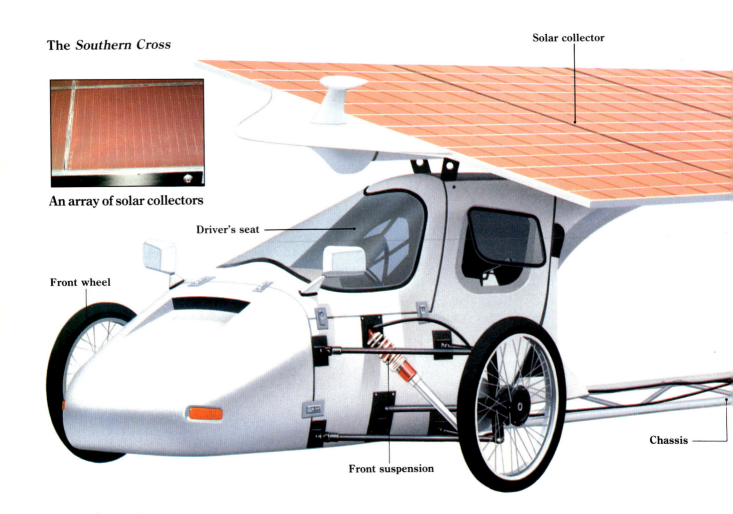

An array of solar collectors

Solar collector

Driver's seat

Front wheel

Front suspension

Chassis

Gears and collectors

Electricity generated in the panel's solar collectors flows over wires to a storage battery. From there, the electricity powers an electric motor that drives the axle and the wheels. A special 12-speed gear system ensures efficient use of energy in a variety of road conditions.

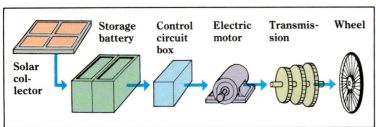

Solar collector — Storage battery — Control circuit box — Electric motor — Transmission — Wheel

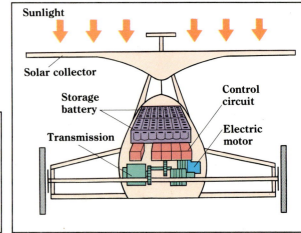

Sunlight

Solar collector

Storage battery

Transmission

Control circuit

Electric motor

The *Southern Cross* has a tiltable solar panel.

The solar battery

Each solar cell has two layers of silicon: a P, or positive, layer and an N, or negative, layer. When light hits the cell it frees electrons in the P layer, producing a current between that and the N layer. The car's motor taps into this current.

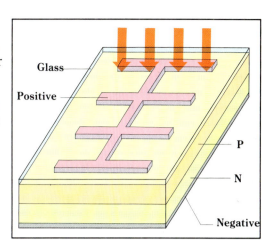

Glass
Positive
P
N
Negative

Japan's *Southern Cross* is about 20 feet long, weighs some 620 pounds, and travels up to about 25 mph on flat surfaces.

Movable panels

To help its solar collectors absorb the most sunlight, the panel can be tilted *(right)* toward the sun, even while the car is moving.

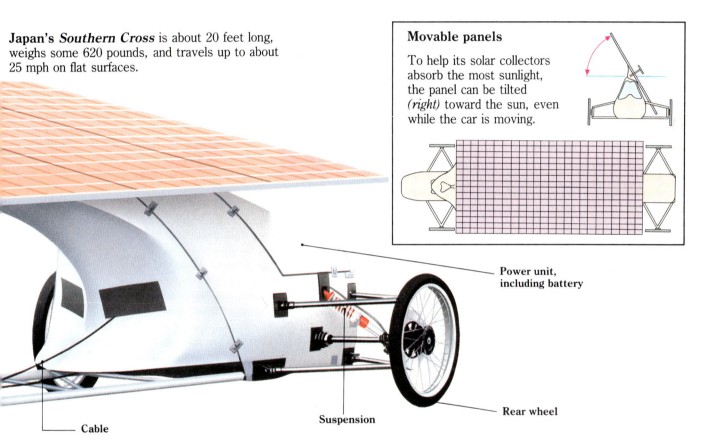

Power unit, including battery

Cable

Suspension

Rear wheel

A streamlined collector panel

The *Solar Flair,* built by a team from Cal Poly Pomona University, competed in the World Solar challenge race in 1990, finishing 11th after racing 1,800 miles across the Australian outback. Twenty feet long, with 9,200 solar cells thinner than a baseball card, it was made of lightweight graphite epoxy and could travel 125 miles on a charged silver-zinc battery without a solar assist.

The Australian race was not without its problems. The bicycle chain drive to the rear wheel broke frequently, often puncturing the tire in the process, slowing the average speed during the race from a predicted 42 mph to an actual 27 mph. With improvements, the car went on to win two U.S. races in 1991.

What Is an Electric Car?

An electric car runs on electricity that comes from an ordinary household socket and is stored in the car's rechargeable batteries. An electric car has no need for the transmission used in cars run by internal-combustion engines. Instead, the electricity goes to an electric motor attached to the drive axle. The motor turns the axle and moves the machine. Already in experimental use, electric cars run about 130 miles before needing a recharge. They are far less polluting and much quieter than petroleum-burning automobiles. Their major drawback is their six-hour recharging time.

Anatomy of an electric car

Steering wheel

Auxiliary battery for headlights, radio

A car with no transmission

The car's controls *(below)* feature the very simplest gearshift lever, because the car has no transmission. Gauges show rpm, speed, and the battery charge.

How electricity turns the wheels

The electricity that powers an electric car is first stored in its batteries *(below, top)*. When the car is running, electricity flows to the electromagnetic connector. Controlled according to data from sensors and the driver's controls, the power is then sent to the motors to turn the wheels and make the car go.

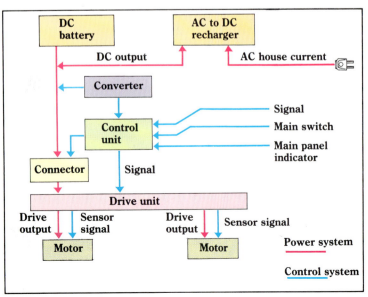

DC battery

AC to DC recharger

DC output

AC house current

Converter

Signal

Main switch

Control unit

Main panel indicator

Connector

Signal

Drive unit

Drive output | Sensor signal | Drive output | Sensor signal

Motor

Motor

Power system

Control system

Recharging a weakened battery

The electric car's recharger, which is used to store a new supply of electrical energy in the car's batteries, draws power from any 110-volt household outlet.

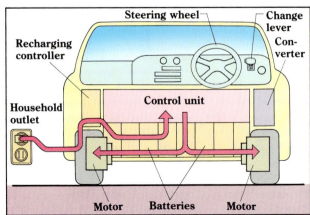

Steering wheel

Change lever

Con-verter

Recharging controller

Control unit

Household outlet

Motor

Batteries

Motor

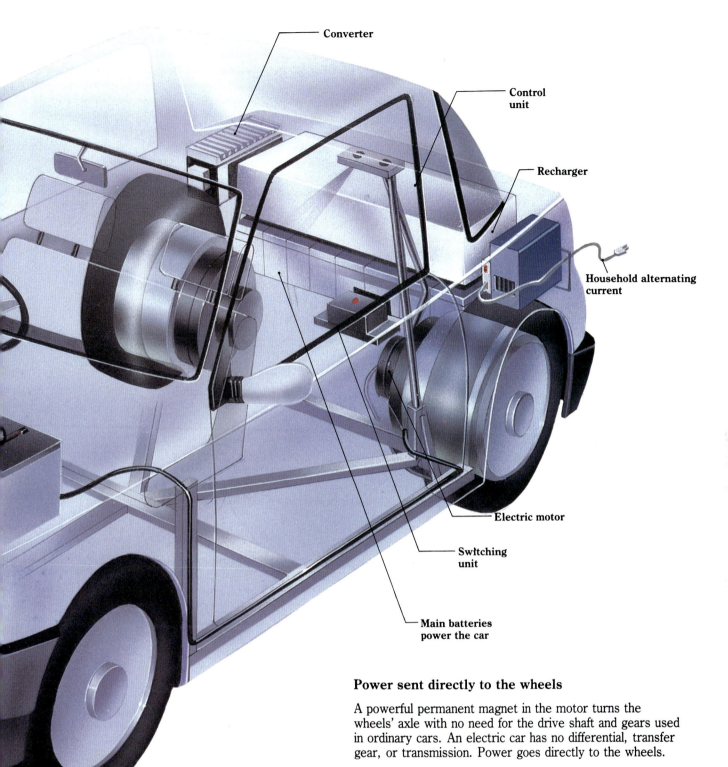

Converter

Control unit

Recharger

Household alternating current

Electric motor

Switching unit

Main batteries power the car

Power sent directly to the wheels

A powerful permanent magnet in the motor turns the wheels' axle with no need for the drive shaft and gears used in ordinary cars. An electric car has no differential, transfer gear, or transmission. Power goes directly to the wheels.

The *Destiny 2000* electric car combines solar panels and batteries with a fiberglass body.

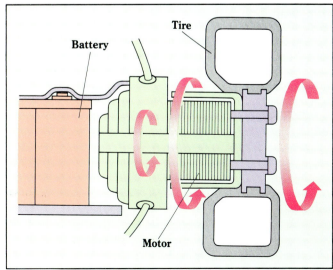

Tire

Battery

Motor

3
A Vehicle for Every Need

Since the invention of the automobile, engineers have found countless new uses for the "horseless carriages," designing vehicles for many different purposes. Vehicles that have rotating tracks or skis instead of wheels, for example, can reach treacherous terrain previously accessible only on foot. A crane was once a cumbersome structure that had to be transported from one construction site to another. With the development of the telescoping boom, a crane mounted on its own movable chassis can now drive easily to building sites where it is used for only a few lifting jobs.

Although the specialized vehicles shown here serve vastly different needs, many have one thing in common: the ability to lift heavy loads. Fire engines hoist long ladders, and cranes and excavators must raise massive booms and their loads. These modern vehicles get their lifting power from hydraulic systems consisting of pistons that fit snugly into oil-filled cylinders. When a pump exerts pressure on the hydraulic fluid, the piston pushes out, moving the ladder or the boom. When the pressure subsides, the piston retracts. The hydraulic systems give these machines a great range of maneuverability. With attachments for digging, lifting, and pushing, these machines carry out ever more complex tasks, as described on the following pages.

The fire engine, snowmobile, and construction equipment in the illustration at right show the range of highly specialized vehicles in use today.

What Makes Snowmobiles Go?

A snowmobile is a motorized sled, powered by an engine similar to a motorcycle's. The snowmobile is steered by handlebars that are connected to a pair of skis at the front. A throttle and brake lever control acceleration and braking. Instead of a rear wheel, a continuous rubber track connected to the engine by gears, a chain, and a belt propels the snowmobile *(right)*.

Snowmobiles are remarkably maneuverable. Not only can they reach speeds of more than 85 miles per hour, but they also climb slopes as steep as 65 degrees. The average car is engineered for a grade only one-third as steep. Because they can travel into areas that are inaccessible to cars, snowmobiles deliver goods and services in frigid regions where the roads are few and often covered with snow. But most people use snowmobiles just for fun.

Drive sprocket

Skis

Continuously variable transmission

Driving on snow

In the engine, pistons turn the primary clutch, which by way of a connecting belt spins the secondary clutch, which is mounted on a jackshaft. On the far end of the jackshaft a gear drives a chain that turns the drive axle. The drive axle's sprockets fit into sockets in the snowmobile's continuous track. As the drive axle rotates, the sprockets force the track forward. Variations in speed, snow conditions, and terrain all call for a change in the amount of energy transferred from the engine to the track. The continuously variable transmission senses these changes and adjusts the power sent to the track, providing a smooth ride.

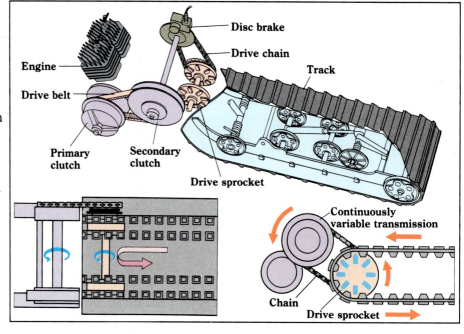

Disc brake

Drive chain

Track

Engine

Drive belt

Primary clutch

Secondary clutch

Drive sprocket

Continuously variable transmission

Chain

Drive sprocket

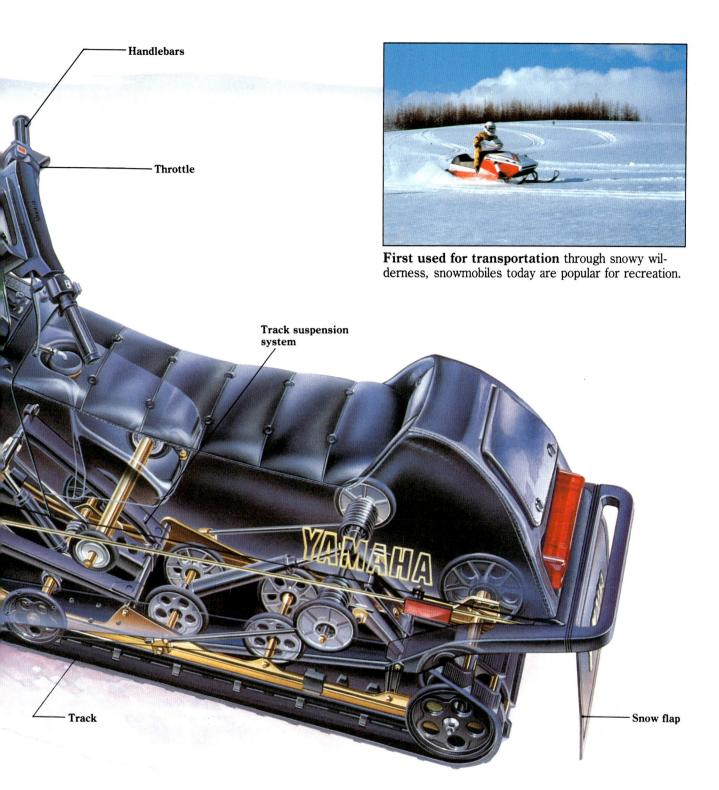

Handlebars

Throttle

Track suspension system

Track

Snow flap

First used for transportation through snowy wilderness, snowmobiles today are popular for recreation.

Steering through the snow

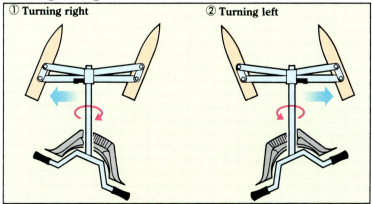

① **Turning right**   ② **Turning left**

A clockwise rotation of the handlebars turns the skis right, while a counterclockwise turn steers left.

Coming to a stop

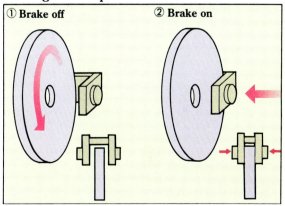

① **Brake off**   ② **Brake on**

When the driver squeezes the brake lever, a set of pads presses against a disk mounted on the jackshaft.

How Does a Fire Pumper Work?

When an alarm sounds, fire trucks race down the road within seconds. The fire pumper, or fire engine *(right),* is the essential vehicle, equipped with pumps that generate powerful jets of water for putting out fires. At the scene of a fire, a pump draws water from a hydrant or a nearby pond or river; then a second pump exerts pressure on the water, forcing it through a fire hose at the rate of 1,000 gallons or more per minute.

Although water extinguishes most fires, water alone is ineffective and sometimes downright dangerous when used against fires caused by oil or chemicals. To douse these types of fires, pumpers use a special foam made by mixing water with flame-retardant chemicals *(far right).*

Fire pumpers can shoot a stream of water farther than 300 feet.

The pumping mechanism

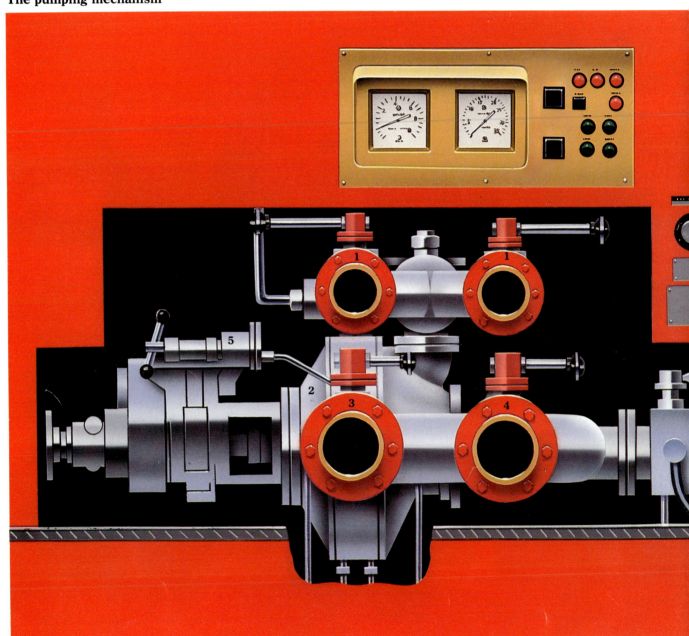

Fighting fires with foam

A mixture of water and flame-retardant chemicals creates a thick foam used to smother fires that cannot be fought with water alone.

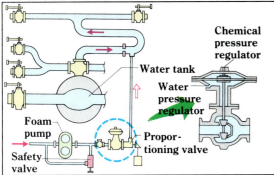

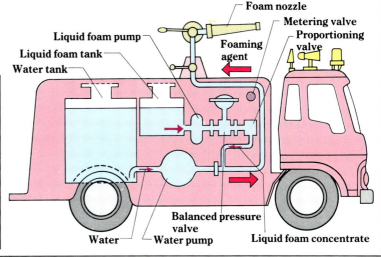

1. Discharge outlet
2. Centrifugal pump
3. Suction intake
4. Auxiliary intake
5. Vacuum pump

Inside the pumper

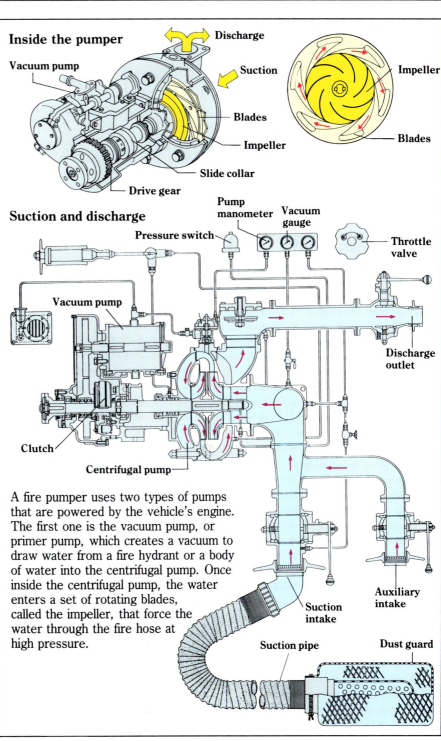

Suction and discharge

A fire pumper uses two types of pumps that are powered by the vehicle's engine. The first one is the vacuum pump, or primer pump, which creates a vacuum to draw water from a fire hydrant or a body of water into the centrifugal pump. Once inside the centrifugal pump, the water enters a set of rotating blades, called the impeller, that force the water through the fire hose at high pressure.

How Do Cranes Lift Heavy Loads?

Cranes extend their powerful arms at every construction site. A mobile crane, such as the one shown below, with a hydraulically controlled telescoping boom, can extend to 130 feet and lift 45 tons of construction materials with ease. When the boom is retracted, the crane becomes compact enough to simply drive away.

A winch controls the cable to which the boom's load is attached. As the winch winds up its cable, the load rises. A system of multiple pulleys and cables between boom and hook reduces the effort needed by the winch to raise a load.

The winch

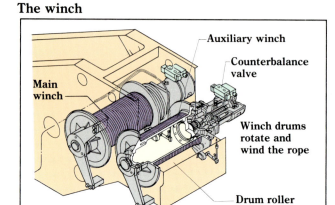

Auxiliary winch

Counterbalance valve

Main winch

Winch drums rotate and wind the rope

Drum roller

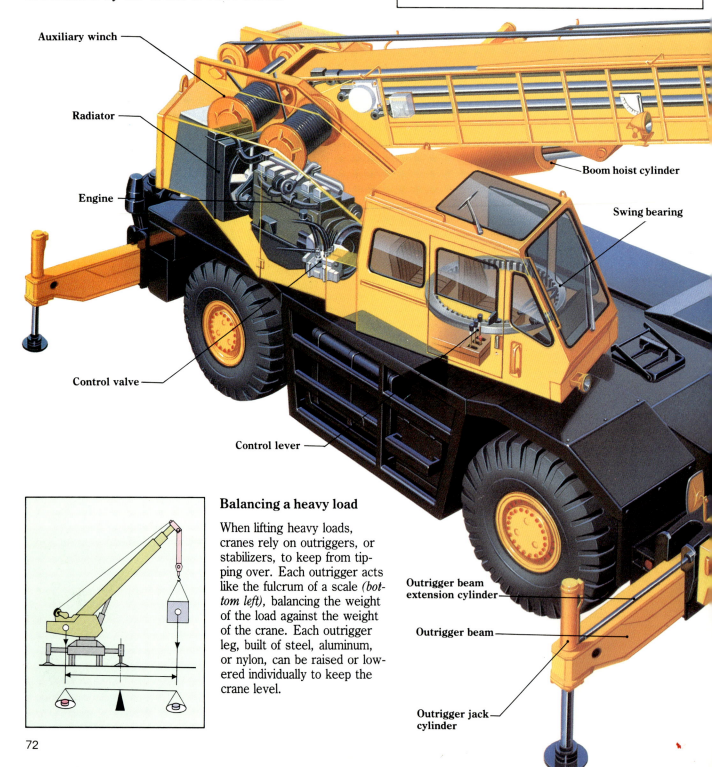

Auxiliary winch

Radiator

Engine

Control valve

Control lever

Boom hoist cylinder

Swing bearing

Outrigger beam extension cylinder

Outrigger beam

Outrigger jack cylinder

Balancing a heavy load

When lifting heavy loads, cranes rely on outriggers, or stabilizers, to keep from tipping over. Each outrigger acts like the fulcrum of a scale *(bottom left)*, balancing the weight of the load against the weight of the crane. Each outrigger leg, built of steel, aluminum, or nylon, can be raised or lowered individually to keep the crane level.

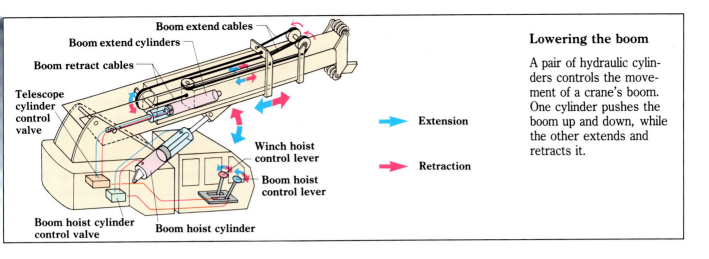

Boom extend cables
Boom extend cylinders
Boom retract cables
Telescope cylinder control valve
Winch hoist control lever
Boom hoist control lever
Boom hoist cylinder control valve
Boom hoist cylinder

→ Extension
→ Retraction

Lowering the boom

A pair of hydraulic cylinders controls the movement of a crane's boom. One cylinder pushes the boom up and down, while the other extends and retracts it.

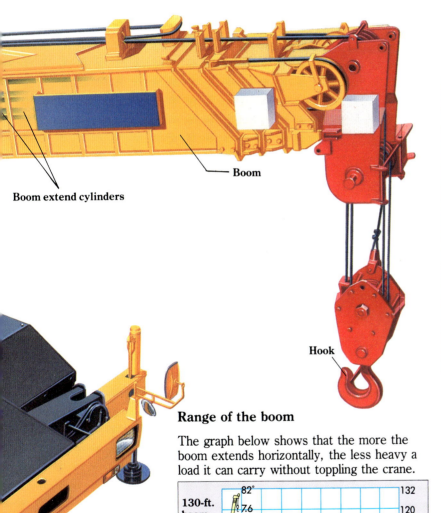

Boom extend cylinders
Boom
Hook

Hook, line, and pulley

Increasing the number of cables and pulleys reduces the effort needed to lift objects.

20-ton-capacity hook block	
4-part reeving	5-part reeving
① ② ③ ④	① ② ③ ④ ⑤

45-ton-capacity hook block	
7-part reeving	11-part reeving

Range of the boom

The graph below shows that the more the boom extends horizontally, the less heavy a load it can carry without toppling the crane.

130-ft. boom
100-ft. boom
80-ft. boom
60-ft. boom
35-ft. boom

82° 7.6 60° 4.7 40° 1.45 20° 0.5 0°
132 120 108 96 84 72 60 48 36 24 12 0
Height (ft.)

14
20
7.1
28 10.5 2.0
20.6 4.0
18 2.1 0.95
4.5 30.2 7.6
45
20.7 6.5

0 12 24 36 48 60 72 84 96 108
Load radius (ft.)

Keeping an eye on the crane

On-board computers keep watch over the crane, monitoring the load, boom angle, boom length, and tilt of the angle of the crane, and sometimes also wind speed.

Screens

KATO ACS

What Does a Construction Roller Do?

A construction roller is a highly specialized vehicle used mainly for paving roads. Instead of wheels or tracks, the machine moves on a pair of steel drums. These drums exert heavy pressure on the ground, compacting the earth into a smooth, even surface. The machines are used in three stages of road construction: First they tamp down a layer of crushed rock, then a layer of finer gravel, and finally the top layer, which is a mixture of asphalt, stone, and sand.

A new type of construction roller is the vibration roller, shown below. Originally, rollers flat-tened road layers solely with their sheer weight. But the vibration roller makes clever use of weights attached to the axles inside the steel drums. As the drums turn slowly, pressurized hydraulic oil from a pump mounted on the engine makes the axles spin quickly, rotating the weights about 4,000 times a minute. The rotation of the weights—which are attached so that most of the weight lies to one side of the axle—causes the rollers to vibrate. These vibrations help pack the layers of rock, gravel, and asphalt more densely than do old-fashioned rollers.

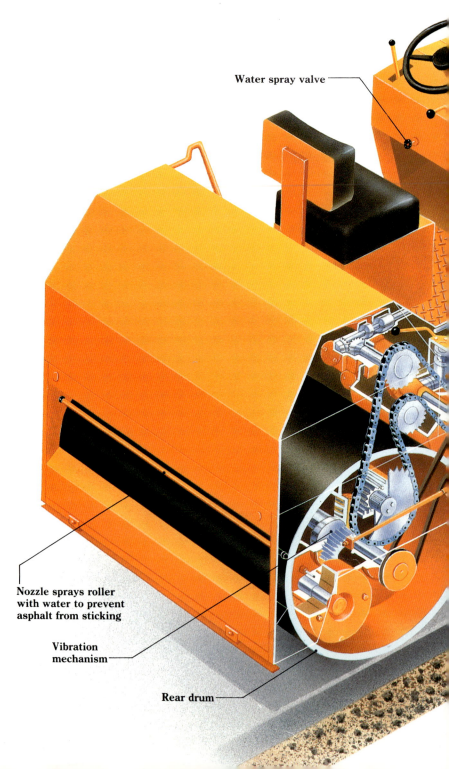

Water spray valve

Nozzle sprays roller with water to prevent asphalt from sticking

Vibration mechanism

Rear drum

Good vibrations

As the rotating weights swing upward, they subtract from the force pressing on the ground. As they swing downward, they add to it. The rapid change in the force applied to the ground sets up a vibration.

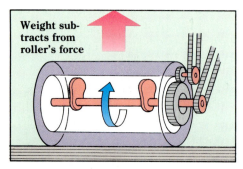

Weight subtracts from roller's force

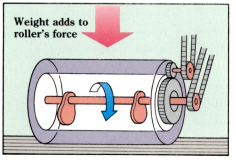

Weight adds to roller's force

A vibration roller tightly packs the surface of a new road.

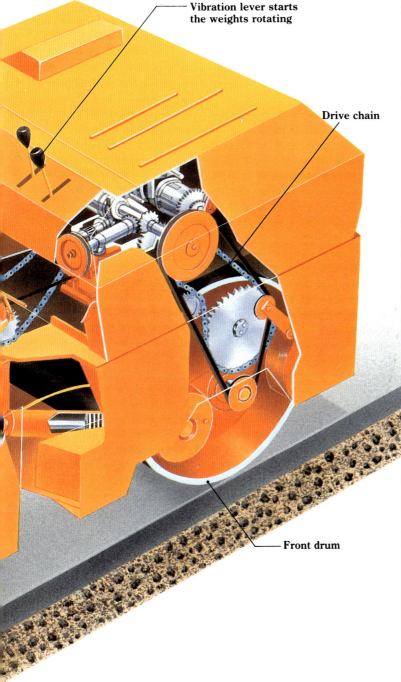

Vibration lever starts the weights rotating

Drive chain

Front drum

Joint vibrations

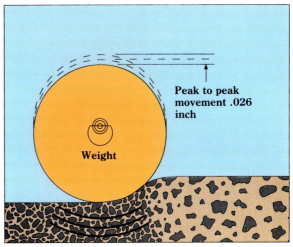

Peak to peak movement .026 inch

Weight

The offset weight inside each drum rotates at a fixed speed. As the weight rotates, it lifts the drum and pulls it up and down while rotating at 4,000 vibrations per minute, all the while packing down the road surface with a centrifugal force of 7,500 pounds. The front drum provides the initial compaction and the rear drum follows in its path, compacting the surface further.

Types of construction rollers

The road roller, a nonvibrational roller, uses its great weight to flatten surfaces.

The tire roller is a specialized roller that uses rows of hard, treadless tires.

What Is a Power Shovel?

A power shovel, or excavator, is a vehicle built for digging, lifting, and dumping material. Moving on rotating tracks similar to tank tracks, these machines use jointed booms that end in buckets for scooping up earth. Many power shovels, such as the one shown below, also have a heavy steel blade attached to the front for leveling terrain.

Like a crane, a power shovel uses hydraulic cylinders to manipulate its boom and bucket. Other hydraulic motors and valves control the motions of the tracks and the bulldozer blade from the cab. The cylinders are powered by the same diesel engine that drives the vehicle.

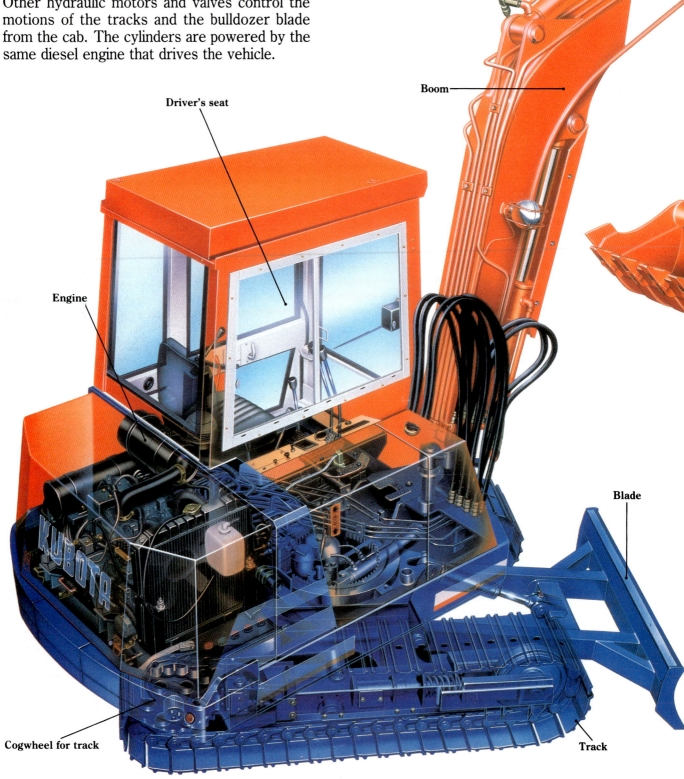

Hoist cylinder

Boom

Driver's seat

Engine

Blade

Cogwheel for track

Track

How a power shovel works

When the engine starts, it activates pumps that push oil into the hydraulic cylinders, causing the boom to extend. The driver controls the motions of the bucket and blade with levers in the cab.

Hoist cylinder
Bucket cylinder
Operation valve
Engine
Boom
Arm
Arm cylinder
Operation valve
Bucket
Cab rotation motor
Oil pumps
Drive motor

Bucket cylinder

Arm

Bucket

Flexing the boom

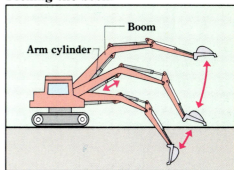

Boom
Arm cylinder

The boom rises as the cylinder piston extends and lowers as the piston retracts.

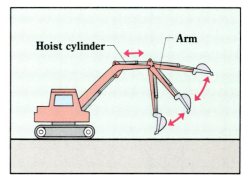

Hoist cylinder
Arm

The arm cylinder piston controls the motions of the arm.

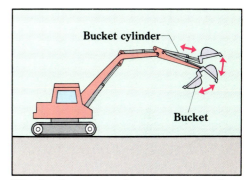

Bucket cylinder
Bucket

The bucket moves inward or outward as its cylinder piston extends or retracts.

At work in a quarry, a power shovel moves rocks and boulders with ease.

Other types of power shovels

The loader uses a large bucket that can be tilted at any angle for loading and dumping.

The bulldozer scrapes and levels construction sites with its front-mounted blade.

The earthmover scoops up earth with a blade mounted under a trailer, then puts the load elsewhere.

4

From Sail to Sub

Humans probably ventured early onto the seas, perhaps limiting their voyages to near-shore jaunts. But in time, science advanced; lore about winds, currents, and storms accumulated; and sailors began undertaking more ambitious transoceanic journeys, steering by the stars. An explosion in global navigation took place in the 15th and 16th centuries, with European explorers and traders extending their routes around the globe. Aided by tools such as the astrolabe and the compass, these travelers ushered in the golden age of sailing ships, during which nations seeking wealth and power vied for mastery of the seas.

By the end of the 19th century, sails were being replaced by engines. The first commercially successful machine-powered ship, the *Clermont,* steamed up the Hudson River from New York City in 1807. Steam eventually gave way to oil. Some military ships are now powered by nuclear fission, the same sort of energy used in certain power plants. Modern navigators turn to advanced technologies that rely on radio, radar, sonar, and laser transmissions to help them safely pilot everything from tugboats to supertankers. The near future promises to bring ships that will be able to travel at ever-faster speeds with increasing efficiency.

The seas have hosted a huge range of vessels, including *(clockwise from near right)* hovercraft, clipper ships, military cruisers, hydrofoils, submarines, motorboats, submersibles, and steamships.

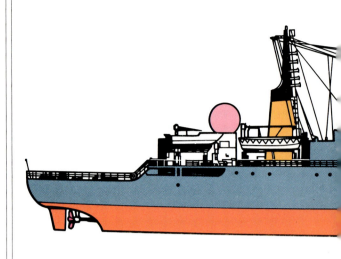

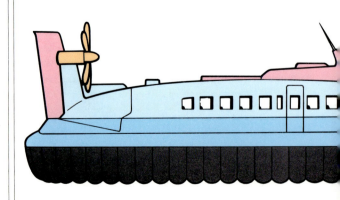

How Do Ships Navigate?

Navigators rely on a number of different tools to find the position of ships at sea, including gyrocompasses, speedometers, charts, and depth sounders. Working with detailed navigational charts, a near-shore sailor sets a desired course from one point to another. Then he or she watches bottom depths, forward motion, and compass heading, adds in the effects of tides and currents, and scans the shore for identifiable features from which to take bearings. Based on these ever-changing data, the sailor adjusts course, as illustrated here. Some sailors can navigate using the stars, but more often they use modern radio direction-finding devices or even newer satellite-based systems that offer accurate readings even in fog or high seas.

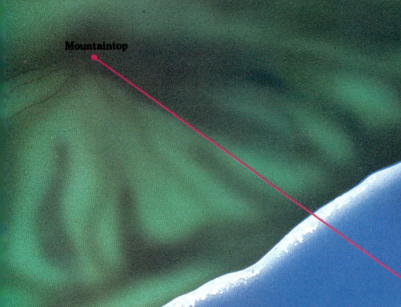

Island

Lighthouse

Mountaintop

N

Adjusted course

A gyrocompass gives a ship's heading versus true north. Bearings are taken by sighting across the dial.

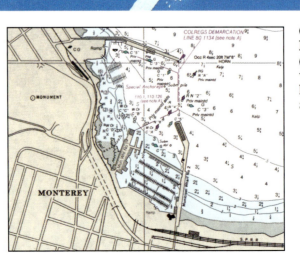

MONUMENT

MONTEREY

Charts, such as this one of Monterey Bay, California *(left),* reveal the depth of the water, navigational aids, and hazards such as wrecks, coral reefs, or sunken rocks.

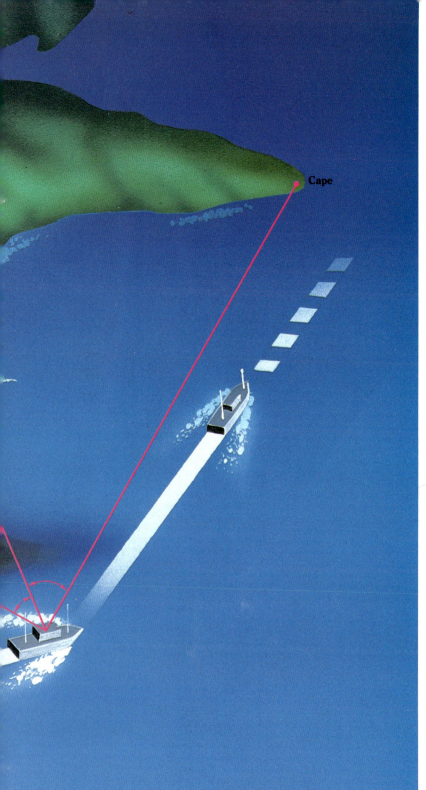

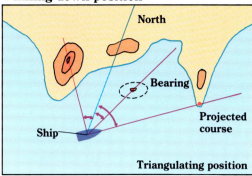

Pinning down position

North

Bearing

Projected course

Ship

Triangulating position

The pilot plots a projected course on a chart, then sights two bearing lines. The lines cross at the ship's approximate location.

Plotting by dead reckoning

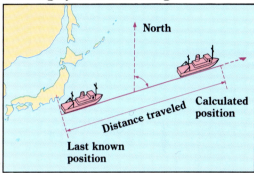

North

Distance traveled

Calculated position

Last known position

Tracking speed and travel time and marking off progress against a projected course yields a rough estimate of a ship's position.

Homing in on radio

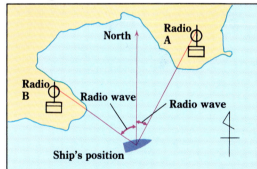

North

Radio A

Radio B

Radio wave

Radio wave

Ship's position

Advanced radio direction finders convert signals from beacons along the shoreline into compass bearings.

Lining up with Loran

Curving lines represent patterns of radio waves generated by a master transmitter at point A and slave transmitters at points B and C. With a special receiver, ships can tune in to such radio signals, generated by a shore-based system known as Loran, short for long-range navigation. To determine position, a receiver compares the arrival times of signals from the stations. Navigators used to consult manuals and perform calculations to plot position. (In the case at right, the ship has been determined to lie at point P.) Newer-model Loran devices automatically provide longitude and latitude.

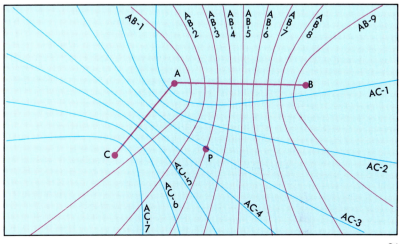

Cape

How Do Ships Navigate in Fog?

Pea-soup fogs and cloudy nights used to be a serious problem for sailors who looked to the shore or sky for guidance. But modern radar and sonar equipment sees through the thickest clouds, allowing ships to proceed with confidence.

By timing reflecting radio waves, radar devices find objects within a given distance of a ship and produce a visual map of them. Depth finders use ultrasonic pulses, bouncing them off the seafloor to measure water depth in feet or fathoms (1 fathom equals 6 feet). Together with position-fixing Loran devices, these mechanical "eyes" provide constant feedback. Although visibility may be zero, the navigator will be able to avoid reefs and islands, locate channels, and give other vessels plenty of sea room.

Sounding the depths

A sonar depth finder, or echo sounder, emits sound pulses and measures how long it takes for them to return. A computer multiplies this round-trip time by the speed of sound—about 4,950 feet per second in water—and divides that in half to calculate the distance to bottom, which is displayed in feet or fathoms.

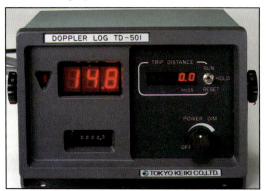

A modern echo sounder shows a reading.

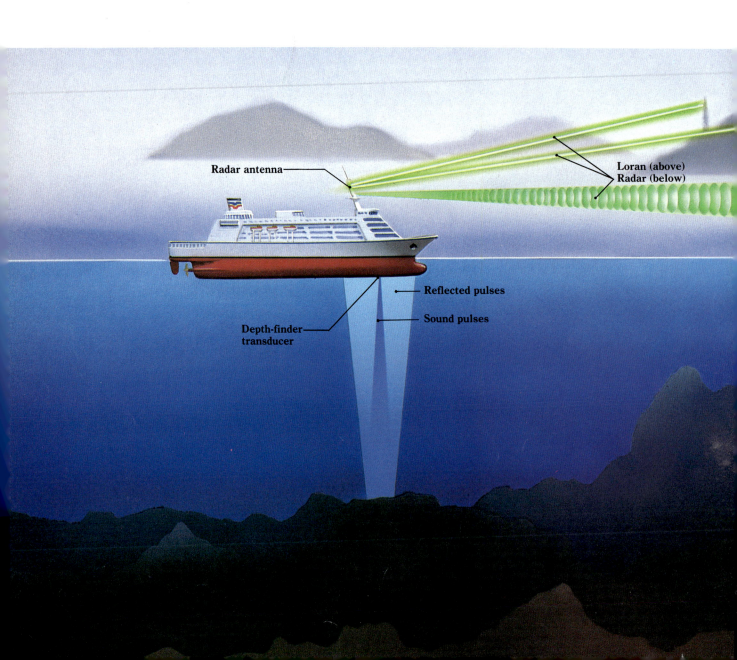

A machine with a bird's-eye view

Even under the murkiest conditions, radar gives navigators detailed views of a ship's immediate surroundings. As the radar antenna *(left)* rotates, it sends out a burst of radio signals, then listens for their echoes *(below, left)*. By reading the blips, an experienced radar operator is able to form a mental picture of landforms, ships, and other objects around the ship. Unfortunately, radar does not echo off of sailboats or fiberglass boats very well, so the pilots must always be alert to their surroundings.

A sweep radar antenna sits below red horns.

Blips appear on a radar screen.

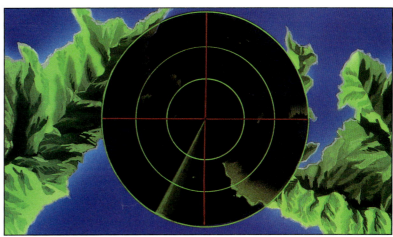

Rules of the sea lanes

Besides instruments, navigators have a standard set of codes that help them avoid collisions. For instance, ships must display running lights of specific colors in certain positions, shown below, so that their heading and orientation can be immediately seen.

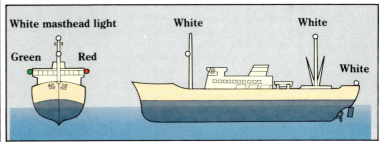

In crowded ports and bays, ships follow universal rules for passing and granting right of way. Ships converging head-on or at an angle must both veer to the right. A ship overtaking another must sound its horn and pass on the side with more room.

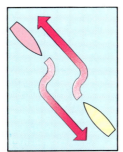

Approaching head-on, each ship turns to starboard.

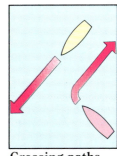

Crossing paths, one ship veers behind the other.

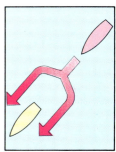

An overtaking ship passes on the less-crowded side.

How Does Satellite Navigation Work?

Circling the globe, navigation satellites send out continuous streams of radio signals. These satellites, which belong to the U.S. Naval Navigation Satellite System (NNSS) and, more recently, the Global Positioning System (GPS), enable ships at sea to determine their location with great accuracy, day or night.

Basically, an NNSS or GPS radio receiver on board a ship snags incoming radio waves, which are broadcast at specific frequencies by the satellites. These signals feed into an attached computer. The computer decodes the signals, gaining information about time of transmission and location of the satellite in its orbit. (These data are beamed to NNSS satellites by ground stations, whereas GPS satellites have their own clocks and tracking instruments on board.)

The computer then finds the distance between the ship and the high-flying satellite. Readings are taken at several intervals and ultimately provide enough measurements for the computer to calculate the longitude and latitude.

Navigating by the NNSS network

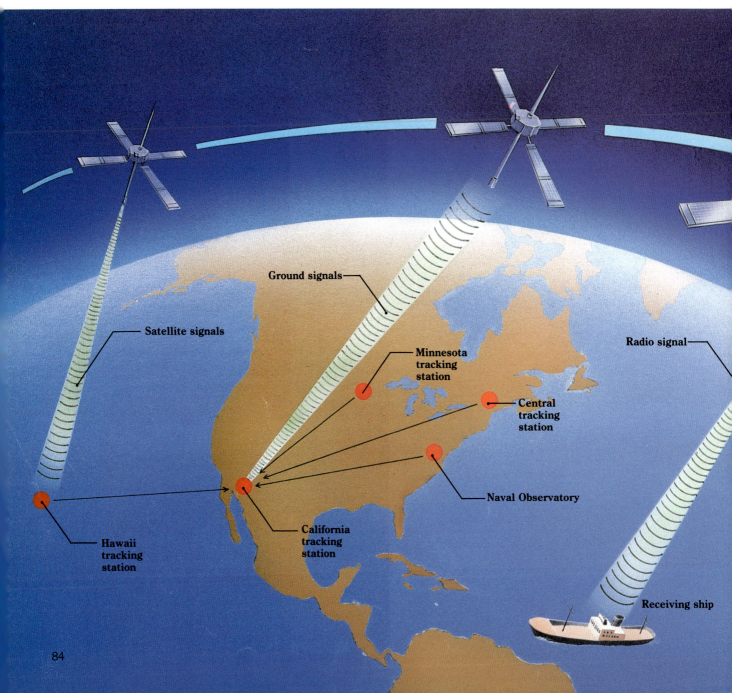

Ground signals

Satellite signals

Minnesota tracking station

Central tracking station

Radio signal

Hawaii tracking station

California tracking station

Naval Observatory

Receiving ship

Solving a problem in orbital geometry

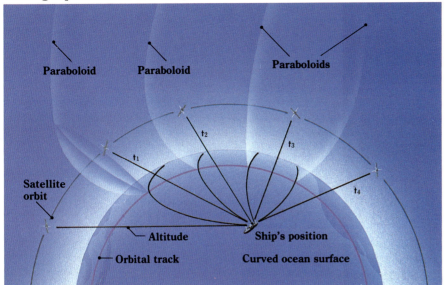

Paraboloid   Paraboloid   Paraboloids

Satellite orbit

Altitude   Ship's position

Orbital track   Curved ocean surface

Correcting for a spherical globe

Ships usually lie some distance away from a satellite on a curved Earth. To correct for this, computers project curved (parabolic) lines from altitude points C1 and C2 and a halfway point between the two. The intersection of altitudes and parabolic lines, P, marks the ship's true position.

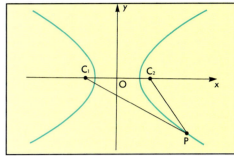

In essence, a moving satellite and radio beams sent out at intervals (t1-t4) trace imaginary pie wedges in the sky. Knowing the length of an arc section of orbit and the lengths of two legs of the wedge, it is possible to calculate the vertex of the wedge—that is, the receiver's location. Adjustments are made for the Earth's curvature (see above).

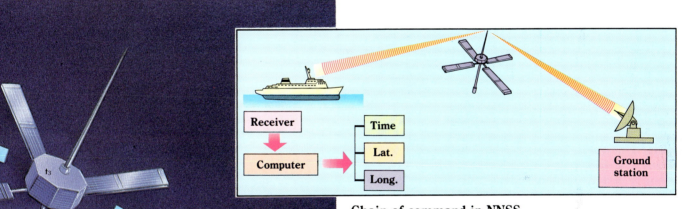

Receiver → Computer → Time / Lat. / Long.

Ground station

Chain of command in NNSS

Time and orbital data beam from a tracking station, above right, to a satellite, which relays signals to a receiver. A computer uses these to calculate longitude and latitude.

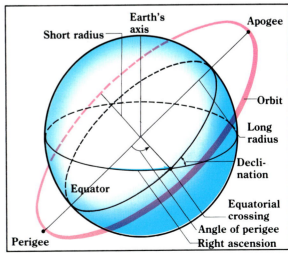

Earth's axis   Apogee

Short radius

Orbit

Long radius

Declination

Equator

Equatorial crossing

Angle of perigee

Perigee   Right ascension

Tracking satellites

Satellite trackers must know a satellite's longest radius, average radius, degree tilt of the orbit off the Earth's axis, lowest altitude (perigee), and time of perigee, among other facts.

How Did Ships Navigate in the Past?

Before modern satellite and computer technology, sailors ventured onto the world's oceans armed with a number of clever devices. One of the oldest of these, the astrolabe, was simplified from an Arabian astronomical instrument for use at sea. Its dials and pins were a means of measuring angles between the horizon and the sun or other celestial bodies—angles that could be translated into terrestrial latitude.

The cross-staff, quadrant, and sextant, invented from the Middle Ages through the Renaissance, were simpler and more accurate, and gradually replaced the astrolabe. Compasses with calibrated dials, perfected in the 11th century, allowed sailors to steer by directional headings. By the 1400s dead reckoning had also evolved. Chips attached to long lines with knots at specific intervals were dropped overboard while a sandglass marked time, thus giving a rough measurement of a ship's speed.

Astrolabe

Quadrant

Reading latitude

The medieval sailor established latitude, or position with regard to the equator, by looking to the sun and stars. The angle of elevation of a given body was measured by an astrolabe *(near right)* or a quadrant *(middle right)*. The sailor then consulted a chart called an ephemeris to determine where the ship was.

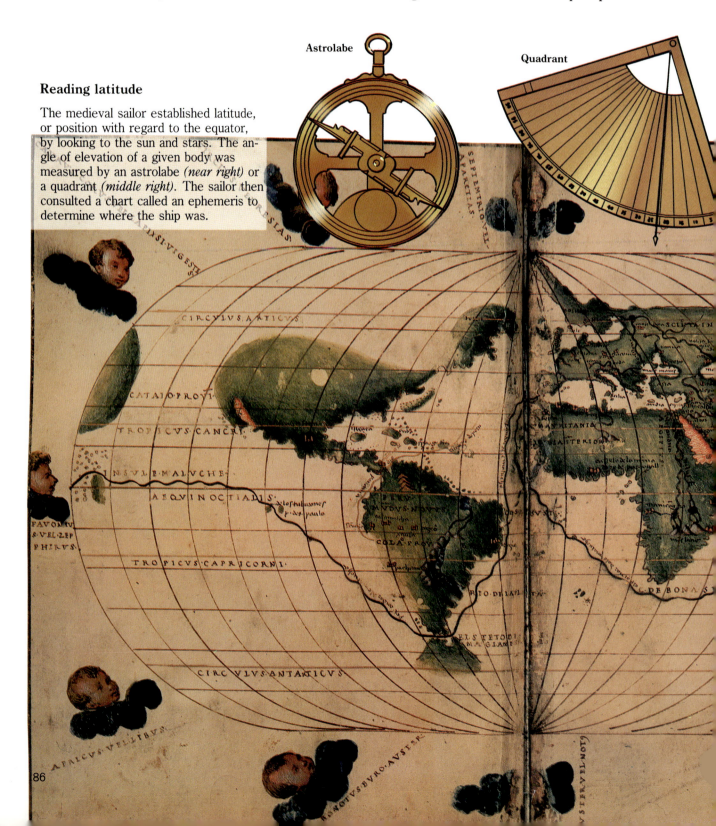

Guessing longitude

Navigators tried to estimate longitude with the help of sandglasses and heavy, knotted lines. The sand slipping through the glass gave a reading of elapsed time, while the line, played out from a reel on the ship, measured speed. Multiplying the day's travel time by the speed gave the total distance traveled. Knowing the ship's starting point and its progress each day, pilots could get a very rough gauge of east-west movement.

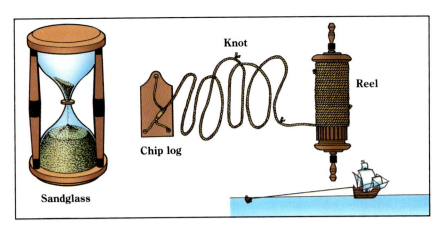

Knot

Reel

Chip log

Sandglass

A medieval compass

Fixed to a painted circular card, an iron needle swiveled atop a central pin, pointing always to Earth's north magnetic pole.

Measuring celestial altitude

To find the altitude of a heavenly body, a navigator would look along a metal cross-staff to the target, then slide transoms of different lengths toward his eye and measure down to the horizon. The shaft was marked with altitudes.

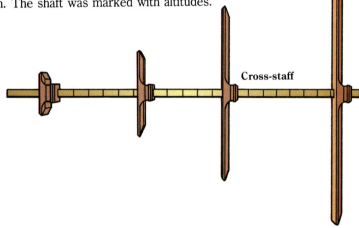

Cross-staff

The ship illustrated below returned home to Portugal in 1522, having carried Ferdinand Magellan's crew on the first expedition around the world. Their route is traced by the wavy line on the 1543 map at left.

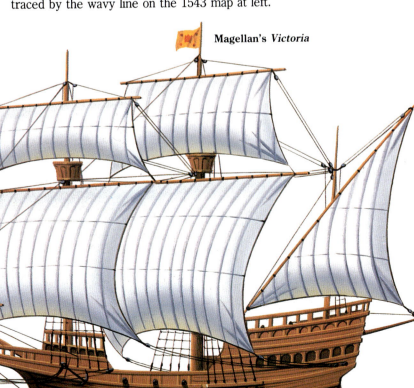

Magellan's *Victoria*

What Was Columbus's Ship Like?

Exact diagrams of Columbus's lead ship, the *Santa Maria,* have been lost to history, but descriptions of similar craft give scholars an idea of its appearance. It was probably a carrack, a type of round-bottomed, high-bowed trading vessel rigged with three masts and a bowsprit extending at an angle from the forecastle, or forward superstructure. Such ships typically had four rectangular sails and flew a triangular lateen sail on the mizzenmast.

The other two members of the expedition, the *Niña* and *Pinta,* were swifter ships called caravels, approximately 70 feet long. After the *Santa Maria* foundered off the island of Hispaniola, Columbus took up the captaincy of the *Niña.*

Basic dimensions

At about 80 feet long and 24 feet wide, the 90-ton *Santa Maria* gained most of its power from mainsails and foresails. It drew 11 feet of water and displaced 233 tons when fully loaded.

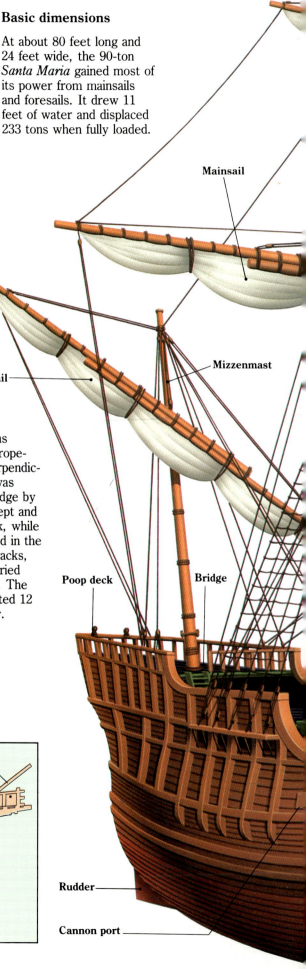

A seagoing vessel

The *Santa Maria* was square-rigged, with rope-lashed sails hung perpendicular to the keel. It was steered from the bridge by a tiller. The crew slept and ate on the main deck, while supplies were stowed in the hold. Like most carracks, the *Santa Maria* carried cannons for defense. The lookout's box projected 12 feet beyond the bow.

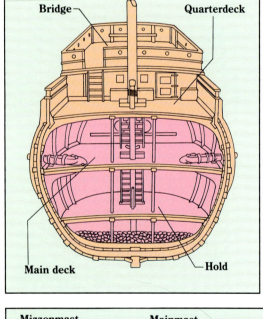

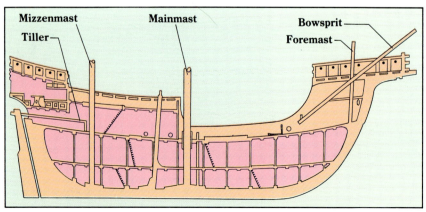

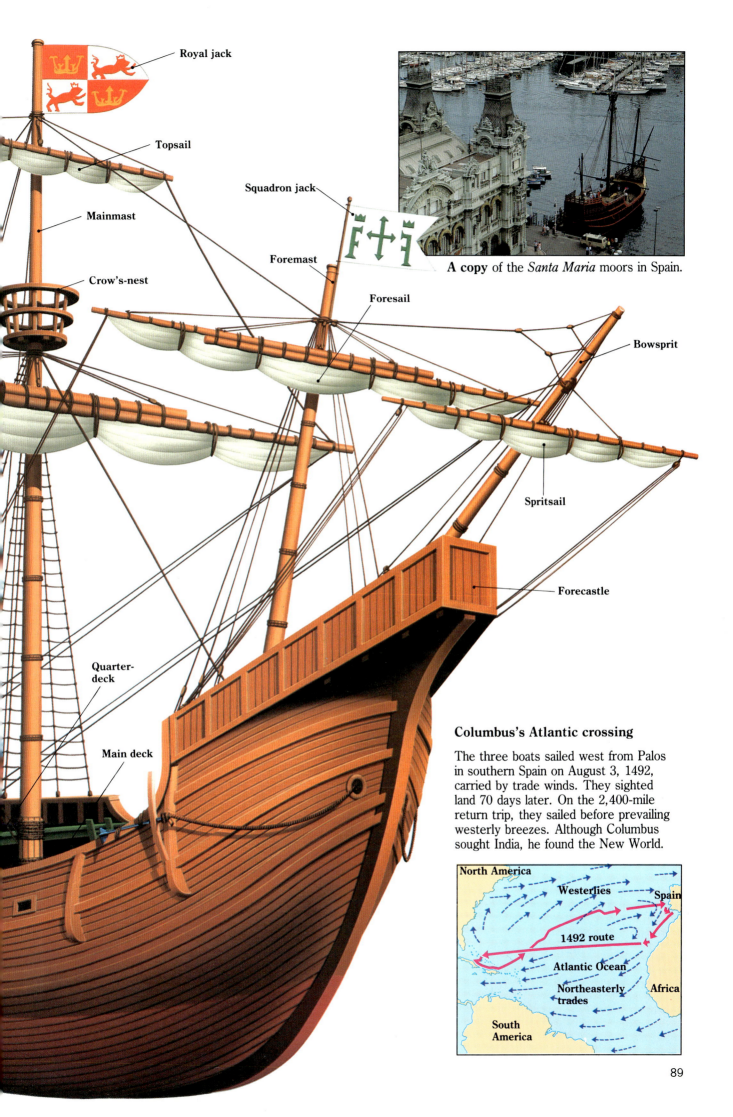

Royal jack

Topsail

Mainmast

Crow's-nest

Squadron jack

Foremast

Foresail

Bowsprit

A copy of the *Santa Maria* moors in Spain.

Spritsail

Forecastle

Quarter-
deck

Main deck

Columbus's Atlantic crossing

The three boats sailed west from Palos
in southern Spain on August 3, 1492,
carried by trade winds. They sighted
land 70 days later. On the 2,400-mile
return trip, they sailed before prevailing
westerly breezes. Although Columbus
sought India, he found the New World.

North America

Westerlies

Spain

1492 route

Atlantic Ocean

Northeasterly
trades

Africa

South
America

What Were Paddle Steamers?

Inventors had tinkered with using steam to propel ships as early as the 1400s. But the first practical paddle steamer was not built until 1807. New Yorker Robert Fulton fitted a bargelike 100-ton wooden vessel, 133 feet long, with a 20-horsepower steam engine. This engine drove side-mounted wheels 15 feet in diameter, which turned arrays of paddles that struck the water and moved the boat forward. Named the *New North River Steamboat of Clermont,* the vessel made regular runs up the Hudson River from New York City to Albany. In 1839 about 1,000 steam vessels, including single and double side-wheelers and sternwheelers, cruised America's lakes and rivers, free from the uncertainties of dependence upon the wind.

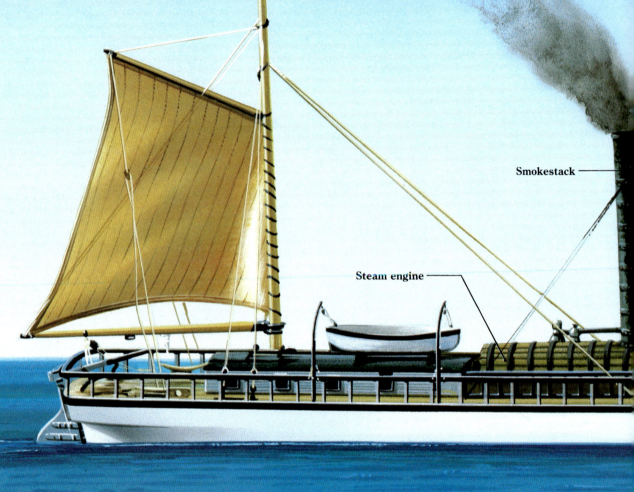

Smokestack

Steam engine

Heat and compression

As perfected by Scottish engineer James Watt in the late 1700s, the steam engine burned wood or coal in a furnace to heat water in a metal boiler. The resulting steam provided the pressure to drive a piston. Rods and cranks translated up-and-down motion of the piston into circular motion, turning the wheel's axle and the attached paddles.

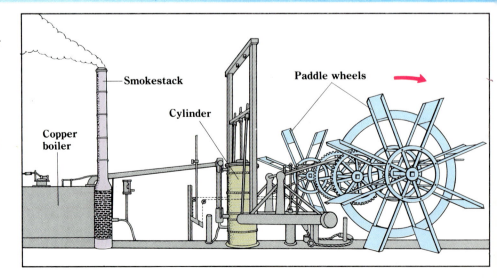

Smokestack

Cylinder

Paddle wheels

Copper boiler

■ Fulton's pioneering craft

The *Clermont,* long and low to the water, made an average speed of 4 knots, or about 5 miles per hour. It undertook its maiden voyage in August 1807, churning 150 miles upstream in 32 hours. Soon thereafter it began providing regular service, ferrying as many as 100 passengers on the overnight trip. The craft boasted cabins as well as berths. Eventually America's first commercially successful steamboat was rebuilt and enlarged, and in its second incarnation plied the Hudson until 1814, when it was retired.

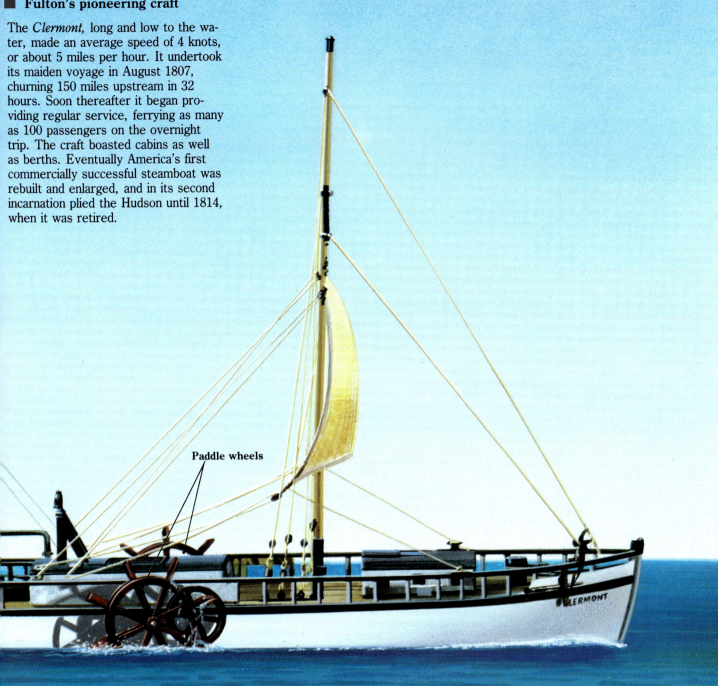

Paddle wheels

Other early efforts

In 1543 a primitive steamboat built by Spaniard Blasco de Galley chugged 6 miles in three hours. But not until the 1700s did the vessels become practical.

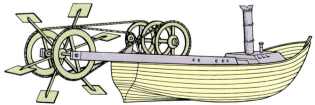

A tugboat patented in 1736 by Britisher Jonathan Hulls was the first to use the motion of steam-driven pistons to turn a wheel at the boat's stern.

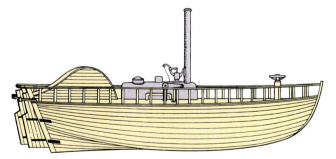

A truly successful steam vessel, the *Charlotte Dundas,* engineered in 1801 by William Symington, towed two canal boats for six hours on its test run in Scotland.

How Does the Panama Canal Operate?

Making runs between the Atlantic and Pacific oceans once involved going around Cape Horn at South America's southern tip, a 7,800-mile circuit. Dug across the Isthmus of Darien between 1881 and 1914 at enormous expense, the Panama Canal allows ships to pass between the Caribbean Sea and the Pacific. It employs a system of locks, or gated chambers which are alternately pumped full of water and drained, to lift vessels up and over the mountainous isthmus. With bow and stern lines, electric locomotives haul ships through each lock.

A tanker heads into Panama's two-way canal.

A major engineering feat

With 50-foot-thick concrete walls and massive V-shaped miter gates, canal chambers work as reservoirs. Water flows in and out through pipes and valves. When the water level in one lock matches that of the next, the steel gates open and the ship proceeds.

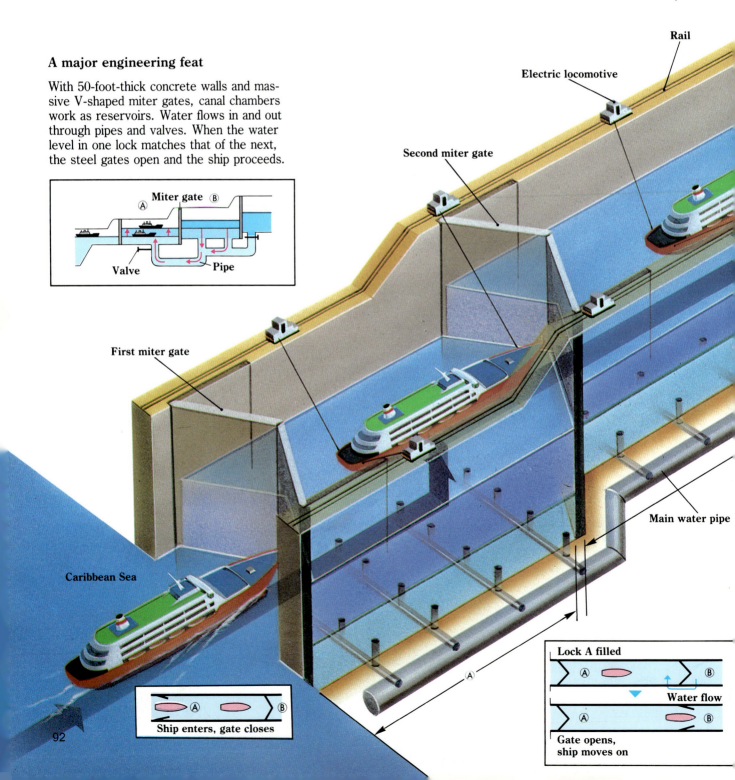

Miter gate Ⓐ Ⓑ

Valve   Pipe

Rail

Electric locomotive

Second miter gate

First miter gate

Main water pipe

Caribbean Sea

Ⓐ

Ship enters, gate closes
Ⓐ   Ⓑ

Lock A filled
Ⓐ   Ⓑ

Water flow

Gate opens, ship moves on
Ⓐ   Ⓑ

92

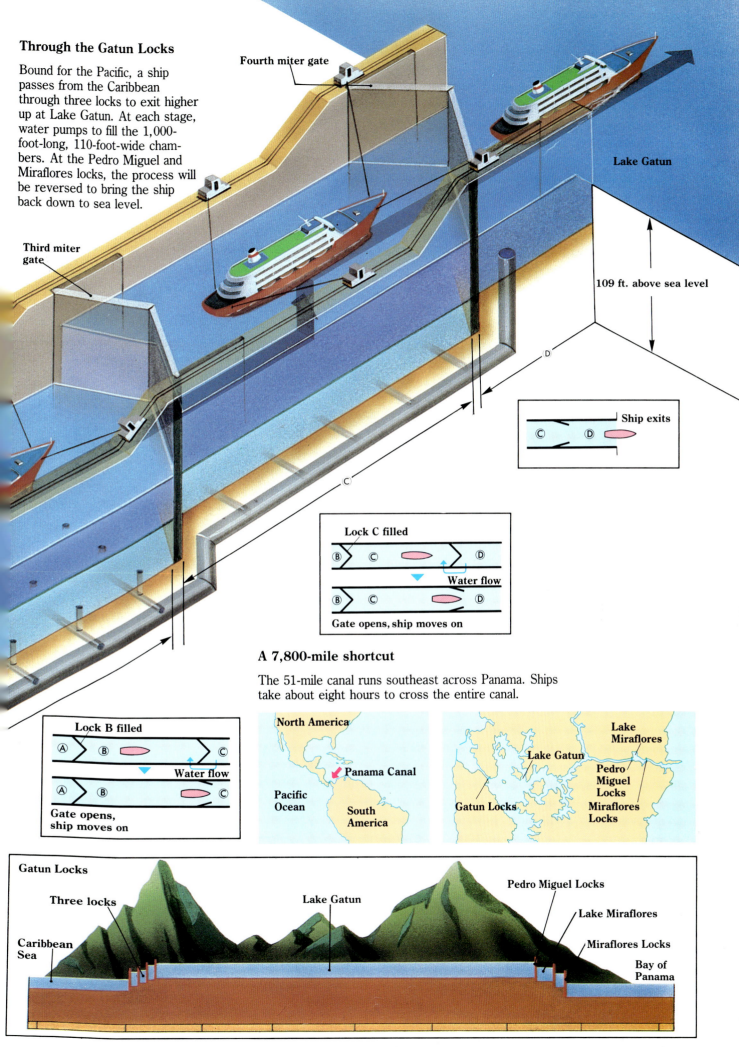

Through the Gatun Locks

Bound for the Pacific, a ship passes from the Caribbean through three locks to exit higher up at Lake Gatun. At each stage, water pumps to fill the 1,000-foot-long, 110-foot-wide chambers. At the Pedro Miguel and Miraflores locks, the process will be reversed to bring the ship back down to sea level.

Fourth miter gate

Lake Gatun

109 ft. above sea level

Third miter gate

Ship exits

Lock C filled

Water flow

Gate opens, ship moves on

A 7,800-mile shortcut

The 51-mile canal runs southeast across Panama. Ships take about eight hours to cross the entire canal.

Lock B filled

Water flow

Gate opens, ship moves on

North America

Panama Canal

Pacific Ocean

South America

Lake Miraflores

Lake Gatun

Pedro Miguel Locks

Gatun Locks

Miraflores Locks

Gatun Locks

Three locks

Caribbean Sea

Lake Gatun

Pedro Miguel Locks

Lake Miraflores

Miraflores Locks

Bay of Panama

How Does a Hydrofoil Work?

As conventional ships approach top speed, both the resistance of waves and the friction of water pouring by the hull increase. To overcome this drag on the hull, the hydrofoil borrows aerodynamic features from the airplane.

Turbine engines drive large waterjet pumps that produce the thrust to drive the boat forward. When the boat reaches speeds of about 30 miles per hour, pressure differences created by foils lift the hull out of the water, reducing drag. Top speed is about 60 miles per hour.

To keep the boat stable and maneuverable, computer-controlled flaps operate on fore and aft foils. Sensors measure the hull's position above the water and gyroscopes measure front-to-back and side-to-side tilt, or pitch and roll. This information feeds into a computer that automatically adjusts the ride. Swiveling the waterjets down or sideways causes the boat to slow or turn.

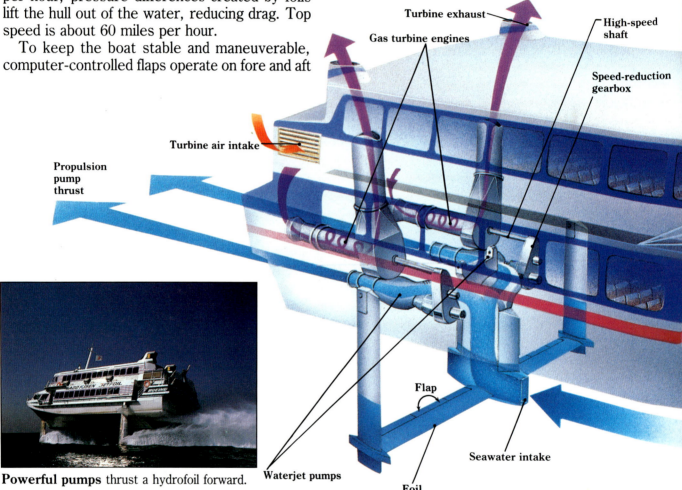

Propulsion pump thrust

Turbine air intake

Gas turbine engines

Turbine exhaust

High-speed shaft

Speed-reduction gearbox

Flap

Seawater intake

Waterjet pumps

Foil

Powerful pumps thrust a hydrofoil forward.

Running in shallow waters

Invented in 1905 by an Italian engineer, the hydrofoil floats at low speeds. In shallow water, the pilot pulls in the aft struts and foils and raises the forward foil.

Forward hydrofoil

Running at high speeds

In deeper waters, the foils are lowered. As the speed increases, the boat's weight moves almost entirely onto the foils, which rise to the surface of the water, buoyed from below.

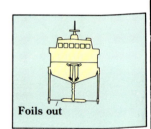

Foils out

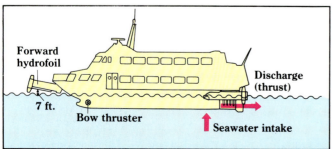

Forward hydrofoil

7 ft.

Bow thruster

Discharge (thrust)

Seawater intake

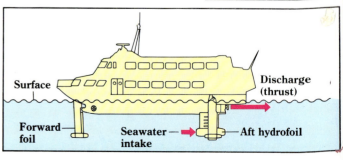

Surface

Forward foil

Seawater intake

Discharge (thrust)

Aft hydrofoil

Powering the pump

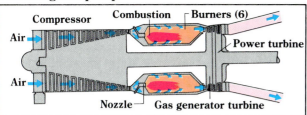

An axial compressor sucks air into the turbine as diesel fuel combusts in six burners. Power passes from the turbine through the shaft and gearbox to drive the pump.

Struts exposed, a hydrofoil flies over the sea.

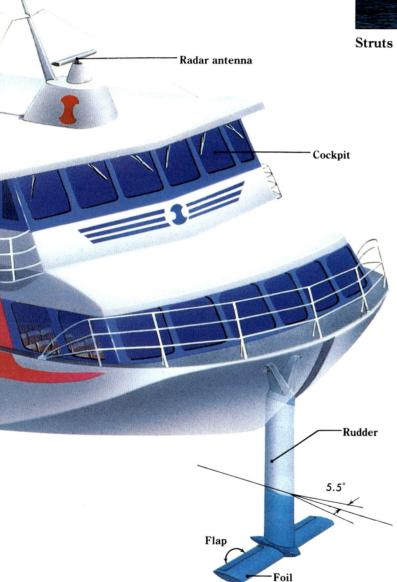

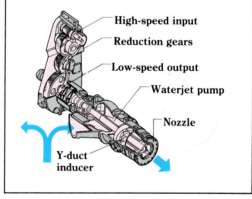

Gearbox plus pump equals thrust

A gearbox slows the turbine's 12,700 revolutions per minute to 2,000. Water flows to the pump's inducer and out jet nozzles.

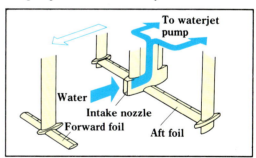

Intake nozzles in the submerged struts supply 24,000 gallons of seawater per minute to waterjets. When the boat is up on foils, seawater filters through a screen into an inlet on the hull.

Computer adjustments on the fly

When up on its foils, the boat is controlled from the cockpit like a plane. A computer adjusts flaps on the foils to increase or lower lift and turns the forward strut to change direction. When floating, the boat turns by deflecting its nozzles right or left, thereby altering thrust. Careful control of the bow thruster allows for sideways motion as the boat approaches or departs the dock.

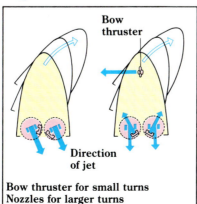

Bow thruster for small turns
Nozzles for larger turns

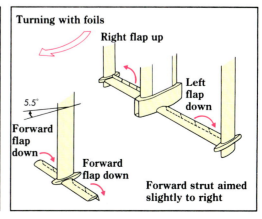

95

What Is a Hovercraft?

Technically, a hovercraft is not a ship but an air-cushion vehicle. At rest, it floats upon the water, but in motion it rides on a cushion of air as much as 5 feet thick, with only its inflated rubber skirt skimming the surface. Fans under the skirt blow hard against the surface of the water to create the cushion, while propellers on deck push the craft forward. Gas turbine engines power both fans and propellers.

Hovercraft can travel on land also, but have found widest use as ferries. The largest reach speeds of 75 mph, almost twice as fast as the fastest ships. However, hovercraft are not stable enough to brave high seas or winds.

Riding the waters on air

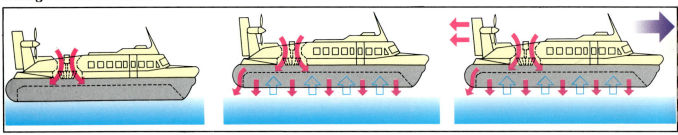

Air sucked into lift fans is blown toward the water and trapped by the inflatable skirt.

The cushion of compressed air lifts the hovercraft, leaving only the rim of the inflated skirt touching water.

Rearward thrust from propellers at the stern translates into the forward motion of the hovercraft.

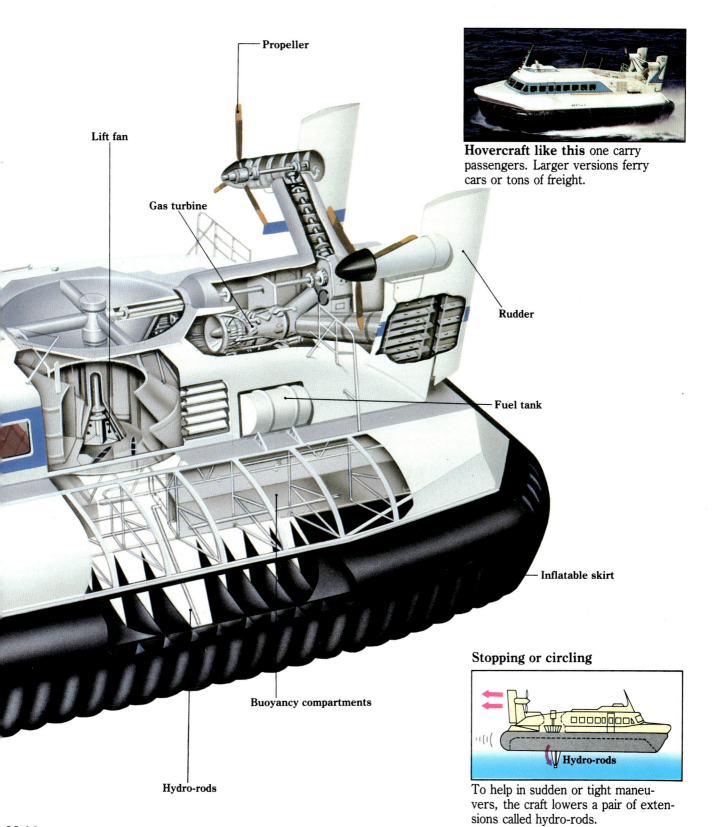

Propeller

Lift fan

Gas turbine

Rudder

Hovercraft like this one carry passengers. Larger versions ferry cars or tons of freight.

Fuel tank

Inflatable skirt

Buoyancy compartments

Hydro-rods

Stopping or circling

Hydro-rods

To help in sudden or tight maneuvers, the craft lowers a pair of extensions called hydro-rods.

Making turns

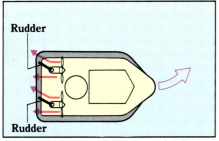

Rudder

Rudder

In motion, the craft turns with its rudders. Pointing them left swings the bow to the left, or port.

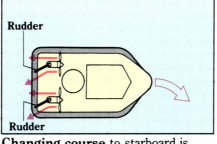

Rudder

Rudder

Changing course to starboard is accomplished by aiming the rudders to the right.

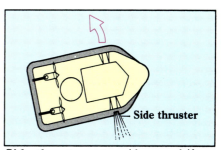

Side thruster

Side thrusters stop sideways drift, or yaw. Above, a thrust from starboard shifts the nose to port.

How Do Submarines Dive and Surface?

Although submarines float easily, they are able to dive to the ocean floor and cruise there for, in some cases, months on end. The secret lies within the sub's unique double-hulled construction. Special compartments, or ballast tanks, between outer and inner hulls can be flooded with seawater, increasing the ship's overall weight and reducing its buoyancy, or ability to float. Thrust forward by the propeller and steered downward by horizontal rudders called hydroplanes, the ship sinks.

The submarine's steel inner hull is designed to withstand enormous pressures that build with depth. Once submerged, the ship is kept steady by trim tanks along the keel. To surface, the sub empties, or purges, its ballast tanks of water. Periscopes, radar, sonar, and satellite networks are the ship's main navigational tools.

British Royal Navy sub *Upholder*

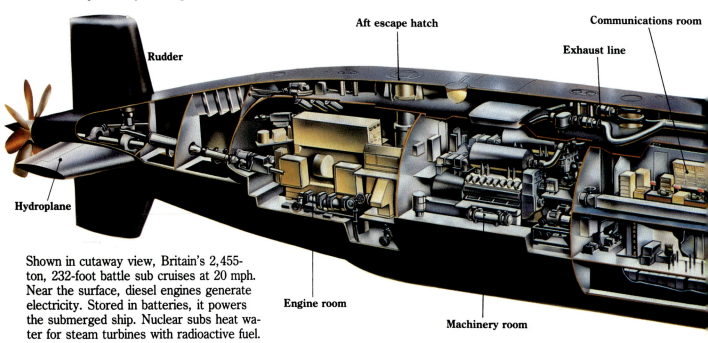

Shown in cutaway view, Britain's 2,455-ton, 232-foot battle sub cruises at 20 mph. Near the surface, diesel engines generate electricity. Stored in batteries, it powers the submerged ship. Nuclear subs heat water for steam turbines with radioactive fuel.

Diving and sounding

Afloat on the surface, a sub is said to be in a state of positive buoyancy, its ballast tanks mostly filled with air (*near right*). When diving (*middle right*), it gains negative buoyancy as the air is expelled through vent valves and water is taken in through flood ports. To cruise at a steady depth below the surface, the sub uses a balancing technique whereby compressed air is forced into the tanks and the flood ports are left open, a state called neutral buoyancy. Rising to the surface (*far right*) requires emptying the tanks of water using compressed air, which is carried on board.

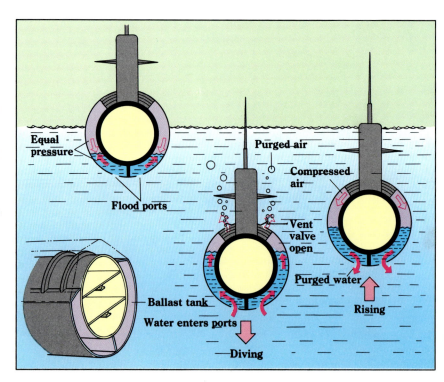

Exhaust snorkel

Air snorkel

Room is scarce inside a submarine. Above, sailors eat in the ship's mess. An American sub surfaces, above right. At right, the cramped quarters where submariners sleep.

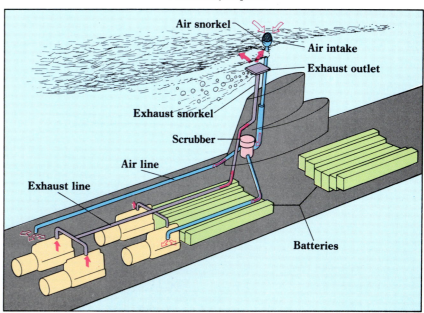

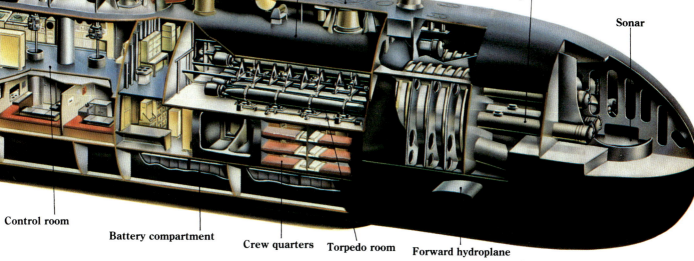

Outer hull

Inner hull **Forward escape hatch**

Torpedo tube

Sonar

Control room

Battery compartment

Crew quarters **Torpedo room**

Forward hydroplane

Fresh air below water

The most sophisticated subs make their own fresh water from seawater. They also produce supplies of air by electrolysis, a process that frees oxygen from fresh water. When cruising near the surface, subs can take in air and release exhaust through lidded snorkels that open above the water line. Along with the periscope, radio antenna, and other masts, snorkels rise from the sub's superstructure, or conning tower, shown at right. The air is monitored daily to ensure that oxygen levels are adequate. Air is also passed through a scrubber that removes impurities. Exhaust flows out through separate piping.

Air snorkel

Air intake

Exhaust outlet

Exhaust snorkel

Scrubber

Air line

Exhaust line

Batteries

How Is an Icebreaker Constructed?

Most ships are designed with narrow-decked, V-shaped hulls, nearly vertical bows, and propellers, or screws, driven directly by the engine. But icebreakers have been specially adapted to navigate seas clogged by shifting ice floes and jammed by thick pack ice. These ships are massive, armored with steel that allows them to crack ice up to 35 feet thick without puncturing or crumpling. Their wide, round-bottomed hulls also help defuse these dangers.

Faced with pack ice, the ship's mighty engines shove the spoon-shaped bow up and onto the ice, where the sheer weight of the load is usually enough to force an opening. To generate power for this maneuver, the screw, well protected under the hull, is driven indirectly by an electric motor, which allows the ship to move at extremely slow speeds.

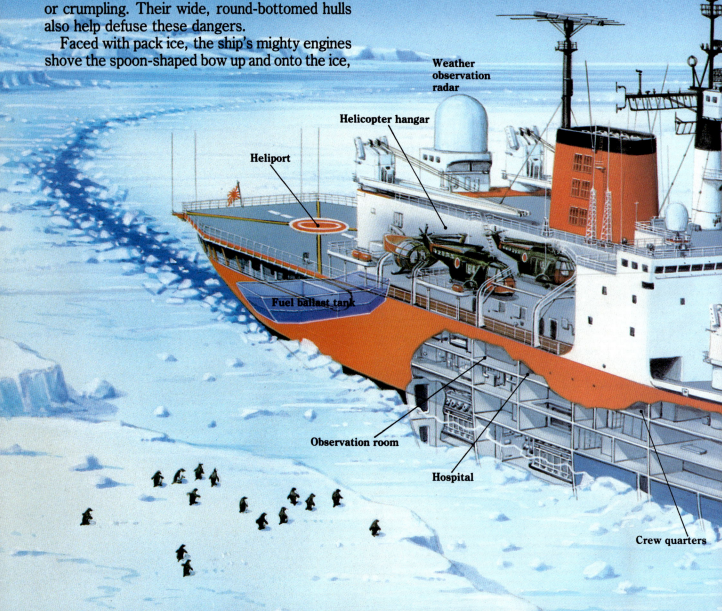

Weather observation radar

Helicopter hangar

Heliport

Fuel ballast tank

Observation room

Hospital

Crew quarters

Strategies for opening sea lanes

The task of opening and maintaining passages to Arctic oil fields, isolated scientific and military outposts, and strategic northern ports falls to icebreakers. Thin ice gives way readily to the mere forward thrust of the weighty ships. When squeezed by floes or widening open stretches further, an icebreaker rocks by moving water between heeling tanks along its hull, as shown at right. The ship's movements shear and shatter flanking ice sheets. Some breakers have side thrusters mounted in the keel to help side-to-side motion.

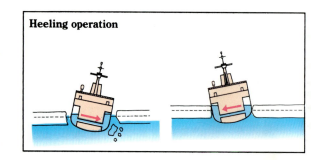

Heeling operation

The 440-foot Japanese icebreaker *Shirase* draws power from three diesel engines harnessed to electric screw motors. Top output totals 90,000 horsepower.

Flying bridge

Crane

5002

Fuel ballast tank

A highly evolved ship

When a pilot sits in the flying bridge, he or she looks down upon a ship that has been made to survive the rigors of polar seas.

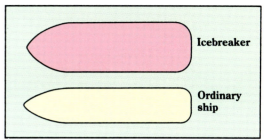

Icebreaker

Ordinary ship

A typical icebreaker is wider, relative to its overall length, than a typical ship. This adds to its stability and increases cargo capacity.

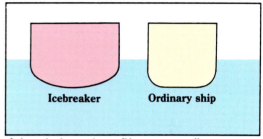

Icebreaker   Ordinary ship

A bowl-shaped profile more easily overrides ice sheets that might trap a conventional ship. It also resists pressure better.

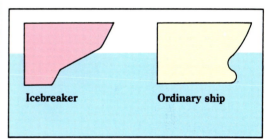

Icebreaker   Ordinary ship

The steeply angled, spoon-shaped bow is designed to slide up onto pack ice, whereas standard bows can only butt the ice.

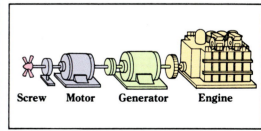

Screw   Motor   Generator   Engine

An icebreaker's engine runs a generator, which feeds electricity to a motor that turns the screw. This gives maximum control over speed.

Meeting pack ice, an icebreaker rams forward, shifting fuel from a fore to an aft ballast tank *(near right).* Once the ship's bow is lodged firmly atop the ice, pumps send the fuel back to the forward tank. The added weight is usually enough to make the ice give way *(far right).*

Ballast tank operation

How Does a Nuclear Sub Work?

Submarines and other nuclear vessels use radio-active fuel, mainly uranium, to heat water into steam. The steam then turns turbine generators to produce electricity for the propulsion system and other equipment on board.

Radioactive materials such as uranium give out heat during a process called fission, in which the unstable central core of an atom, called the nucleus, splits in two, releasing enormous amounts of energy. In a sub, this phenomenon takes place within a reinforced reactor vessel that must be cooled constantly by water to prevent overheating, or meltdown. Nuclear fuel is favored for military subs and aircraft carriers because of its tremendous efficiency. On a single golf-ball-size piece of uranium, a submarine can circle the globe seven times. However, nuclear power also poses hazards, not only to crews under threat of runaway reactions, but also to sea life, which can be poisoned by radioactive wastes.

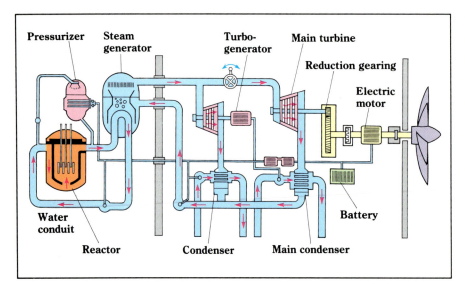

Pressurizer **Steam generator** **Turbo-generator** **Main turbine** **Reduction gearing** **Electric motor** **Water conduit** **Reactor** **Condenser** **Main condenser** **Battery**

Inside the engine

In a typical nuclear engine *(left)*, cool, pressurized water flows into a reactor vessel holding fissioning fuel. Heated water exits the reactor and is used to convert water into steam (it is then recooled and cycled back to the reactor). The steam turns the blades of a turbine engine. Reduction gearing translates the rapid spinning of the turbine into slower rpms for the electric propulsion motor and propeller, both of which require a lower rate of spin. The motor also feeds electricity into batteries for later use.

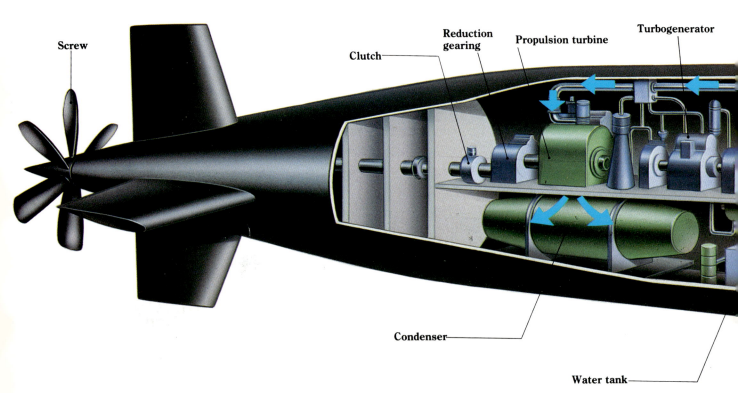

Screw **Clutch** **Reduction gearing** **Propulsion turbine** **Turbogenerator** **Condenser** **Water tank**

A nuclear sub coasts at the water's surface. Such subs need to refuel only every two to three years.

Operators in the conning room keep an eye on the surrounding waters via a periscope. Radar, sonar, radio, and side-scanning cameras also aid navigation.

Making fission happen

Inside a reactor, an atomic nucleus, composed of subatomic particles called neutrons and protons, is struck by a free neutron *(below)*. The nucleus splits, releasing neutrons that bombard other atoms and cause a chain reaction of fissioning nuclei. This releases huge amounts of heat energy.

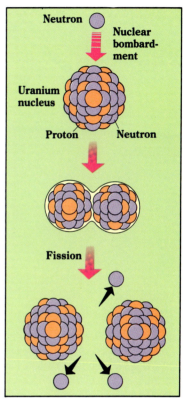

Neutron

Nuclear bombard- ment

Uranium nucleus

Proton   Neutron

Fission

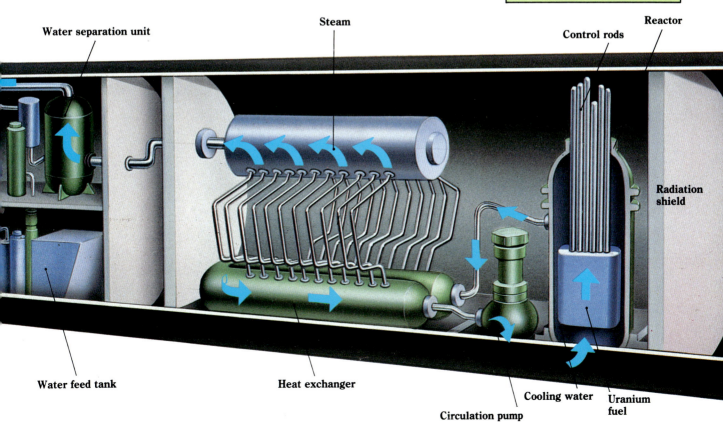

Water separation unit

Steam

Control rods

Reactor

Radiation shield

Water feed tank

Heat exchanger

Circulation pump

Cooling water

Uranium fuel

What Might Future Ships Look Like?

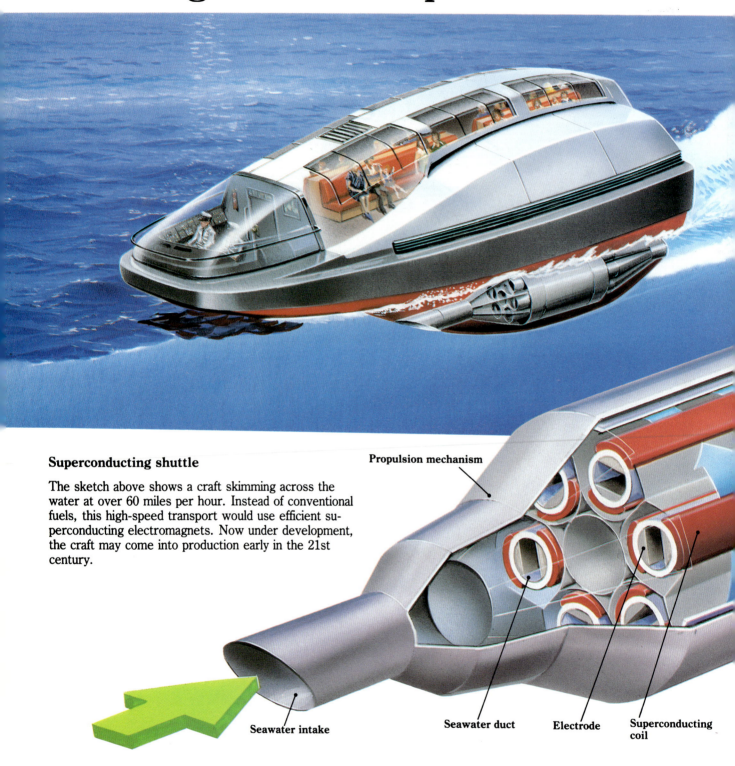

Superconducting shuttle

The sketch above shows a craft skimming across the water at over 60 miles per hour. Instead of conventional fuels, this high-speed transport would use efficient superconducting electromagnets. Now under development, the craft may come into production early in the 21st century.

Propulsion mechanism

Seawater intake

Seawater duct

Electrode

Superconducting coil

Over the next half-century, ships may not look radically different. But engineers are dreaming up superconducting ships like the one above that would make oil- and coal-fueled ships with standard propulsion systems obsolete.

Superconductivity is a physical phenomenon whereby some metallic substances held at extremely cold temperatures offer no resistance to the flow of electricity. Once a current is induced in them, it flows virtually forever, making superconducting devices extremely efficient.

A quest of modern physicists has been to find substances that become superconductive at or near room temperature. However, even before that happens, coolants such as liquid nitrogen might come into play. One proposed propulsion device, in cutaway above, would use superconducting magnets to eject water at high speed from nozzles, creating thrust to drive ships. Such devices would operate with little electricity.

Superconducting propulsion devices

Vacuum
Vacuum chamber
Liquid helium
Super-conducting coil
Electrode
Heat-sealed plate
Seawater duct

Twin propulsion devices under the hull house electromagnets.

In each device, six electromagnets produce a magnetic field.

An electromagnet contains coils and electrodes.

Seawater outlet

Magnetic current

Thrust from electromagnets

Some engineers believe that superconducting propulsion devices will take the place of conventional propellers. In this device, seawater pours into a central duct. Meanwhile, current runs through electrodes, or pairs of wires, inside the device. This in turn causes superconducting coils to generate a powerful magnetic field that expels the water forcefully through jet nozzles.

Magnetic current

Superconducting coil

Magnetic field

Electrode

Magnetic field

Electric current

Electro-magnetic power

Force

Propulsion

Seawater

Electric current

The left-hand rule

This handy method shows the direction of motion produced by electric motors. The left forefinger indicates magnetic field direction, the middle finger direction of current, and the thumb points in the direction of force.

What Is a Deep-Diving Submersible?

■ A deepwater submersible

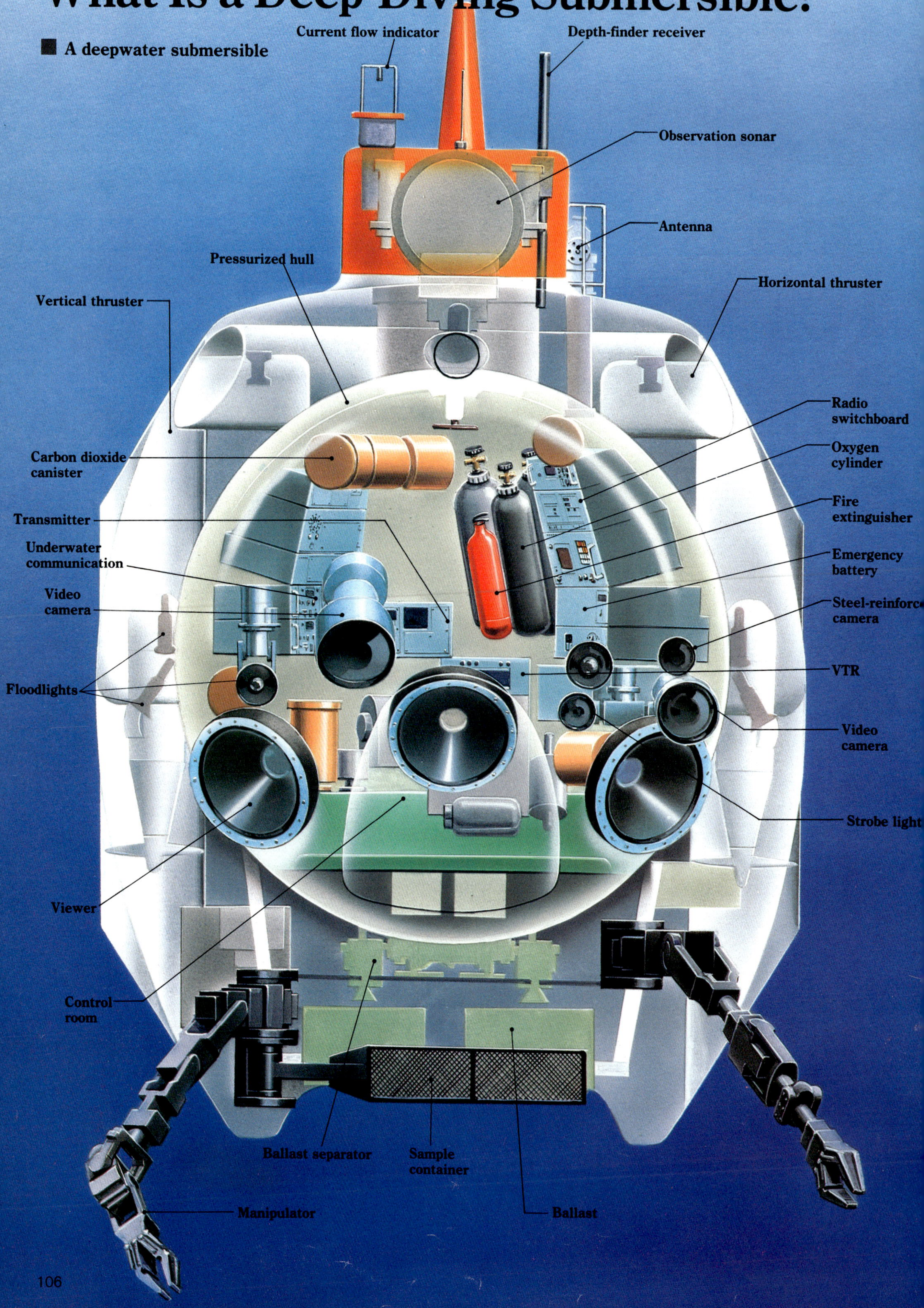

Current flow indicator

Depth-finder receiver

Observation sonar

Antenna

Pressurized hull

Horizontal thruster

Vertical thruster

Radio switchboard

Carbon dioxide canister

Oxygen cylinder

Transmitter

Fire extinguisher

Underwater communication

Emergency battery

Video camera

Steel-reinforced camera

Floodlights

VTR

Video camera

Strobe light

Viewer

Control room

Ballast separator

Sample container

Ballast

Manipulator

Submersibles, including bathyspheres and bathyscaphes, are small, highly specialized submarines that generally serve scientific purposes rather than military ones. Heavily reinforced and often built out of exotic, high-strength metals such as titanium, these tiny vessels have probed the ocean to record depths. In 1960, the French submersible named *Trieste* made the deepest dive ever, descending 35,802 feet to the bottom of the Mariana Trench in the Pacific Ocean.

Operating under pressures as much as 1,000 times greater than at sea level, submersibles scan and photograph the underwater terrain with both still and video cameras. With robotic arms, they collect geological and biological samples which are carried to the surface in mesh bins. The arms can also be used to repair equipment on pipelines or communications cables.

Side view of the submersible

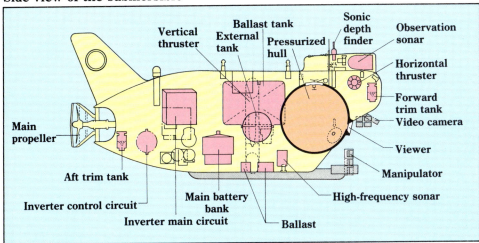

Pressure increases with depth

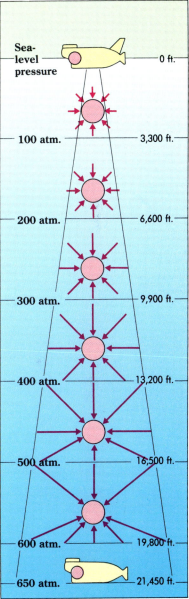

Every 3,300 feet down, pressure rises 100 atmospheres. (One atm. equals sea-level air pressure.)

A bathyscaphe

This bathyscaphe yokes a fortified spherical crew cabin to a large gasoline-filled float. Ballast tanks within the float are filled with seawater for descent and emptied for ascent. On the outside of the bathyscaphe, much of the gear—floodlights, television and 35-mm cameras, strobe lights —is devoted to seeing the lightless depths of the ocean.

The bathyscaphe *Alvin,* above, has helped to pioneer underwater exploration.

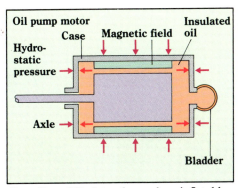

Gasoline-filled tanks and an inflatable bladder diffuse the effects of pressure.

The interior of the *Alvin's* cramped cabin is lined with instruments.

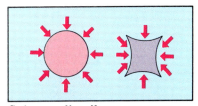

Spheres distribute pressure better than cubes, which are more easily collapsed.

5
Dreaming of the Heavens

Humanity's age-old dream of flight became a reality in 1903 when Orville and Wilbur Wright built a lightweight but powerful engine capable of propelling an aircraft. The Wrights' piston engine, like its modern descendants, worked on the same principle as an automobile engine but used its power to turn propeller blades rather than a drive shaft. Invented during World War II, a second type of aircraft engine, the jet, operates by burning fuel combined with compressed air. The resulting high-temperature gas speeds out in an exhaust stream, which provides thrust to move the aircraft.

Using innovative techniques of design and construction, new materials, and computer technology, modern aircraft dwarf both the size and capabilities of the Wright's first flier. Today's portly jumbo jets carry as many as 550 passengers, while military aircraft reach blazingly fast speeds of several thousand miles per hour. Some aircraft are unusually nimble, able to take off and land without runways, fly sideways, and evade detection by radar. Worldwide traffic control centers guide pilots safely along the correct routes, while on-board navigational instruments keep them informed of their positions even over the widest ocean or in the thickest fog.

The diversity of flight is illustrated at right. Shown (not to scale) are the Wright *Flyer,* a helicopter, a Stealth bomber, a 747 jumbo jet, the supersonic Concorde, various military aircraft, and a lighter-than-air airship.

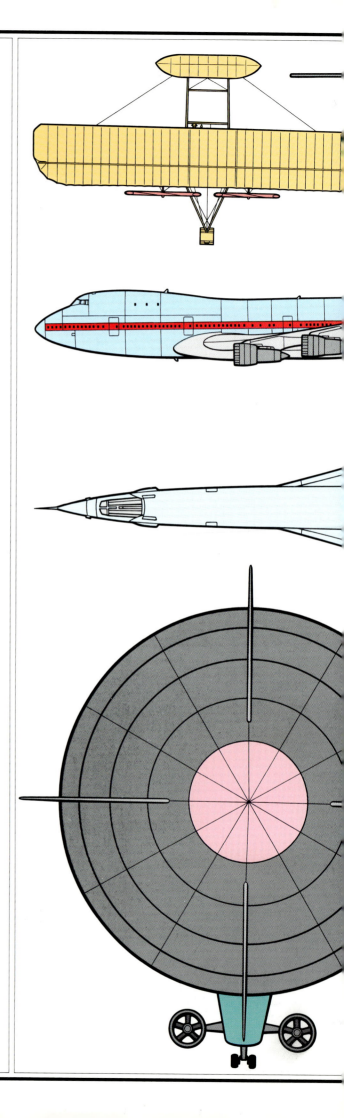

How Does an Airplane Fly?

Airplanes achieve flight through a combination of power from the engines and lift provided by the wings. As an aircraft moves forward, air passes over the wings. The wings are curved in such a way that the upper surfaces are longer than the lower surfaces, so that air passing over the upper surfaces has to move faster. This creates an area of low pressure above the wings. The difference between pressure below and above the wings is called lift. The force of lift increases with speed, eventually overcoming the downward force of gravity. During takeoff, wing flaps are extended to increase wing area and lift. In flight, the aircraft ascends or descends by changing the angle of attack of its wings.

The force of lift

Forces acting on an aircraft

Aircraft are acted upon by the forces of thrust, lift, gravity, and drag.

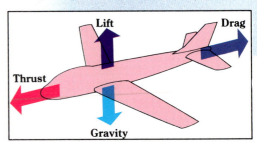

During liftoff, the pilot raises the aircraft's nose and extends wing flaps in order to increase lift.

How lift acts upon the wings

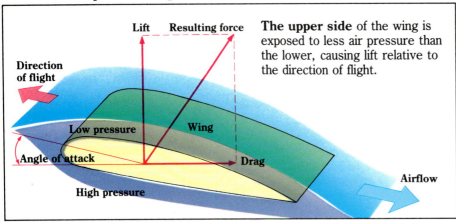

The upper side of the wing is exposed to less air pressure than the lower, causing lift relative to the direction of flight.

Angle of attack and lift

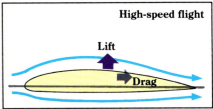

In high-speed flight, angle of attack is low, lift and drag are greatest.

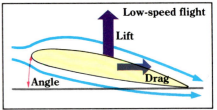

In low-speed flight, angle of attack is about 14°, and lift force is high.

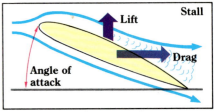

If angle of attack exceeds 15°, a stall may result as turbulence reduces lift.

Function of flaps

To prevent stalling at low speeds, the wing angle must be raised by lifting the nose. Flaps enable the pilot to make this attitude adjustment. Flaps are located in the leading and trailing edges of the wings. When flaps are extended, the area of the wings and the angle of attack are increased, providing increased lift. When not in use, flaps are folded into the wings.

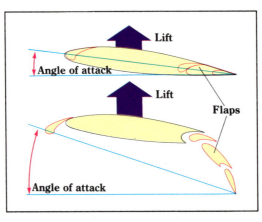

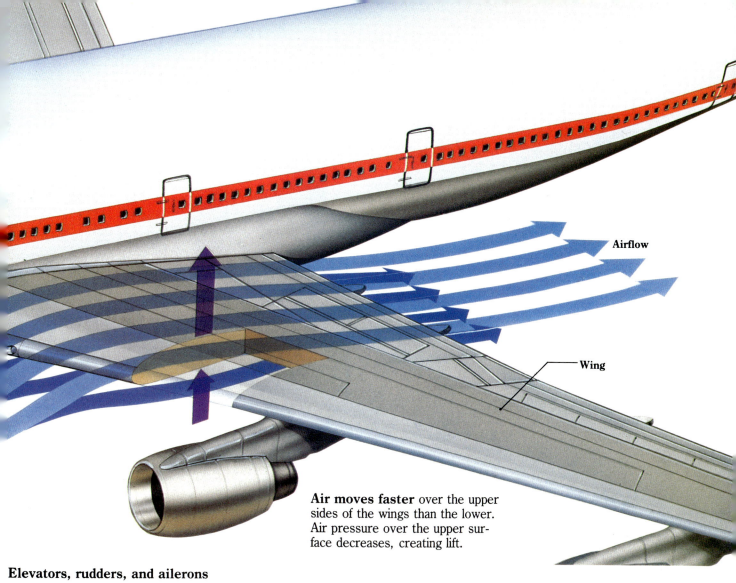

Airflow

Wing

Air moves faster over the upper sides of the wings than the lower. Air pressure over the upper surface decreases, creating lift.

Elevators, rudders, and ailerons

Elevators, located on the trailing edges of the horizontal stabilizers, are used when raising or lowering the nose. The rudder, on the trailing edge of the vertical stabilizer, is used to change the direction of the nose to the right or left. Ailerons, on the trailing edges of the wings, raise or lower the wings during turns.

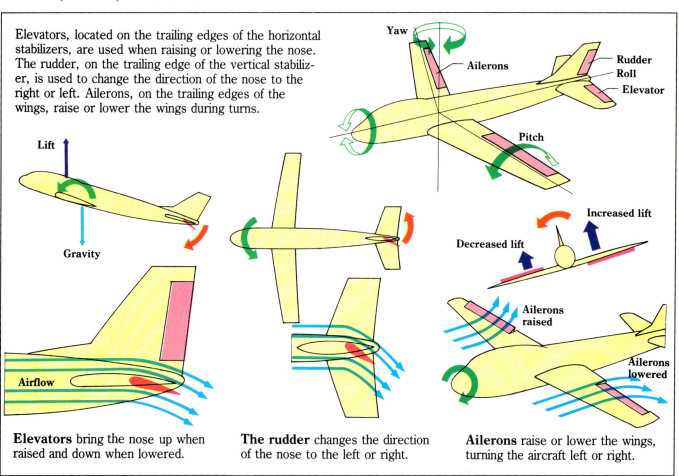

Elevators bring the nose up when raised and down when lowered.

The rudder changes the direction of the nose to the left or right.

Ailerons raise or lower the wings, turning the aircraft left or right.

How Do Propeller Aircraft Work?

Before the development of jet engines, all aircraft used propellers that were driven by internal-combustion piston engines like those in automobiles. Each propeller blade has a cross section shaped like that of an airplane wing. As the propeller rotates, the air current in front of the blades' surfaces travels faster than the air behind them. The resulting low pressure in front of the propeller creates a forward drive force. The amount of force created increases in direct proportion to the rotation speed of the propeller.

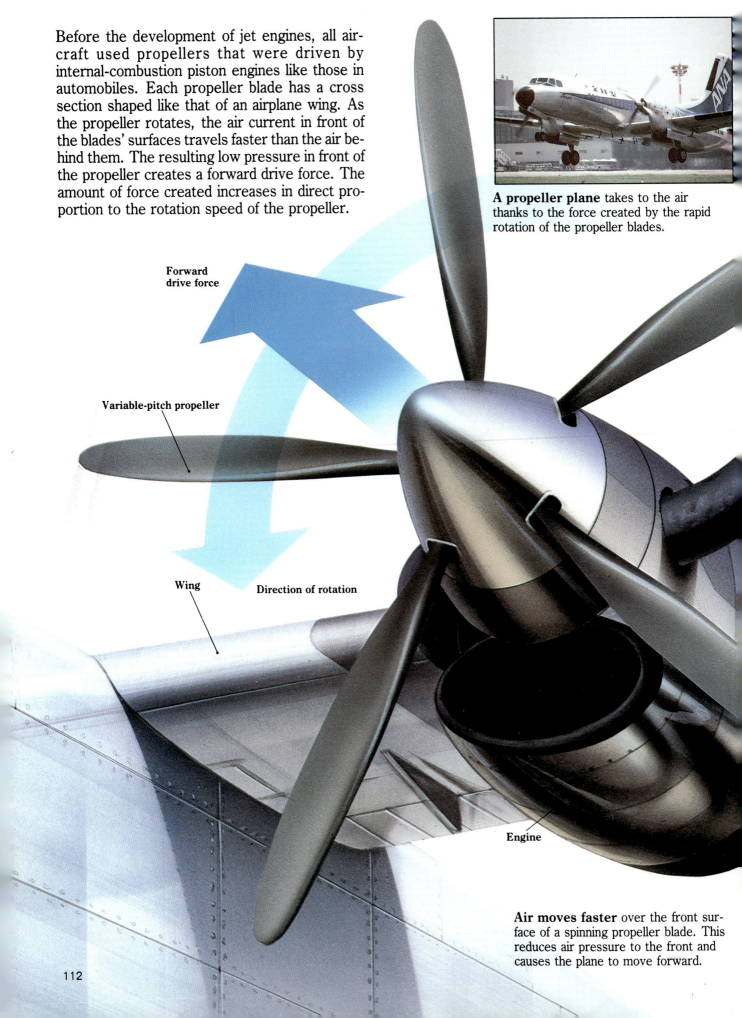

A propeller plane takes to the air thanks to the force created by the rapid rotation of the propeller blades.

Forward drive force

Variable-pitch propeller

Wing

Direction of rotation

Engine

Air moves faster over the front surface of a spinning propeller blade. This reduces air pressure to the front and causes the plane to move forward.

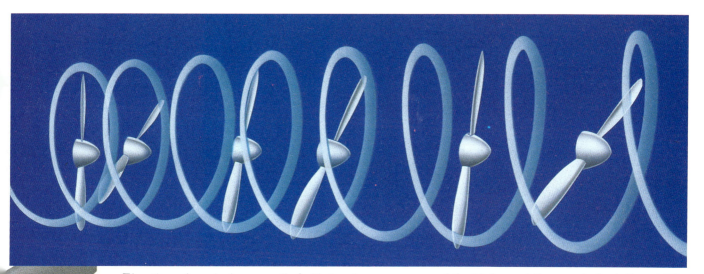

The tips of a spinning propeller's blades describe a spiral through the air. The amount of air handled by the propeller depends on the size of the blades and the speed of rotation. Additional blades and more powerful engines can increase the propeller's efficiency.

Why propeller blades are twisted

If propeller blades were flat, air would be distributed evenly over the blade's surface, creating resistance and drag. Instead, blades are twisted, so that the air current is inclined to the surface, creating a different direction of airflow at different points on the blade. This design allows the blade to cut through the air more efficiently, creating a balance between the forces of propulsion and resistance.

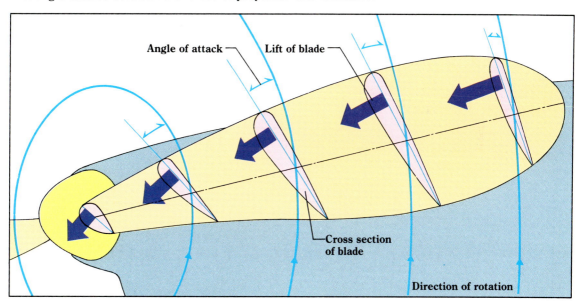

Angle of attack — Lift of blade

Cross section of blade

Direction of rotation

Variable-pitch propellers. The angle at which a propeller blade is installed in the hub is called the pitch angle. In some aircraft, the angle of pitch can be adjusted to provide maximum efficiency in different flying conditions, such as takeoff, climbing, or cruising.

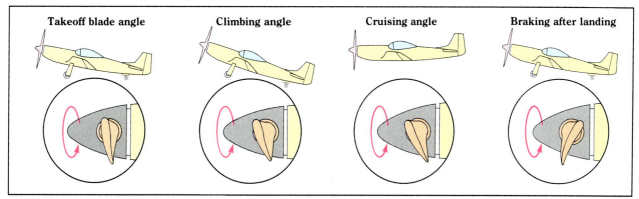

| Takeoff blade angle | Climbing angle | Cruising angle | Braking after landing |

How Does a Helicopter Fly?

Helicopters fly by spinning long rotor blades whose cross sections are like those of airplane wings. The amount of lift provided by the blades can be varied by adjusting the angle of all the blades at once, while turns are executed by adjusting each blade during its rotation cycle. To fly forward or backward, or to the left or right, the spinning rotor tilts in the direction of the motion. A small auxiliary rotor blade mounted in the tail stabilizes the helicopter, preventing it from spinning around with the momentum of the lift rotor. Helicopters can hover motionless in the air by balancing the weight of the aircraft against the lift force generated by the rotor.

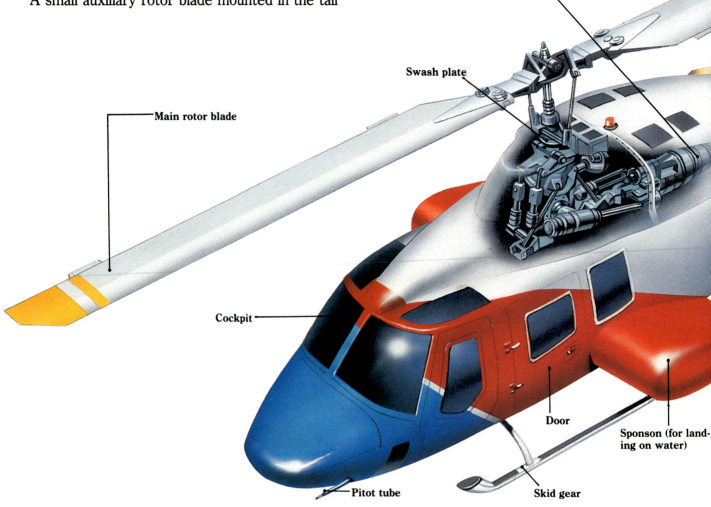

Turbine engine

Swash plate

Main rotor blade

Cockpit

Door

Sponson (for landing on water)

Pitot tube

Skid gear

The main rotor

In cross section, the main rotor blade looks like an airplane wing. Air currents pass over the upper and lower surfaces of the blade, creating low pressure above it and generating lift.

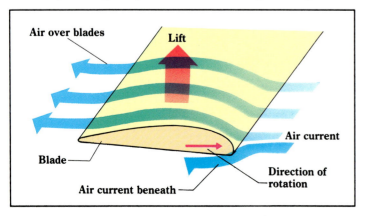

Air over blades

Lift

Blade

Air current

Direction of rotation

Air current beneath

The auxiliary rotor

Force from the main rotor would spin the entire aircraft around if not for the steadying effect of the auxiliary rotor mounted on the tail.

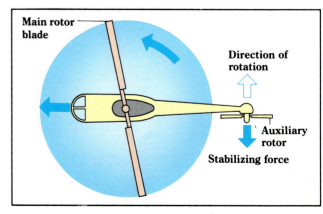

Main rotor blade

Direction of rotation

Auxiliary rotor

Stabilizing force

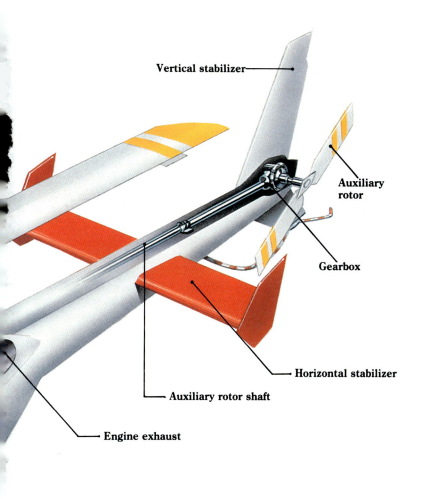

Vertical stabilizer

Auxiliary rotor

Gearbox

Horizontal stabilizer

Auxiliary rotor shaft

Engine exhaust

The main rotor hub

To maintain a steady flight, the pilot must adjust the angle of the rotor blades using a device known as a swash plate, found on the rotor shaft. The helicopter can fly, circle, or hover according to the way the pilot controls the swash plate. As shown below, moving the swash plate up and down changes rotor blade pitch. The swash plate can also be tilted to alter the angle of the rotor's disk.

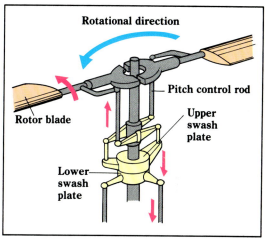

Rotational direction

Pitch control rod

Upper swash plate

Rotor blade

Lower swash plate

Piloting a helicopter

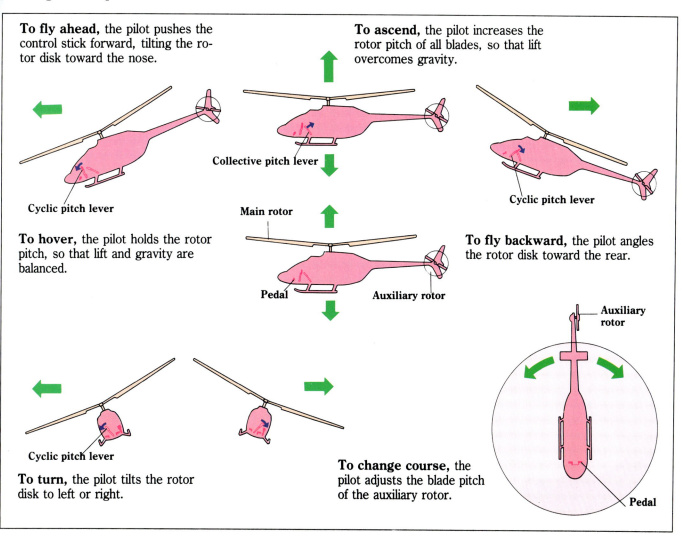

To fly ahead, the pilot pushes the control stick forward, tilting the rotor disk toward the nose.

Cyclic pitch lever

To hover, the pilot holds the rotor pitch, so that lift and gravity are balanced.

To ascend, the pilot increases the rotor pitch of all blades, so that lift overcomes gravity.

Collective pitch lever

Main rotor

Pedal

Auxiliary rotor

Cyclic pitch lever

To fly backward, the pilot angles the rotor disk toward the rear.

Cyclic pitch lever

To turn, the pilot tilts the rotor disk to left or right.

To change course, the pilot adjusts the blade pitch of the auxiliary rotor.

Auxiliary rotor

Pedal

115

What Is an Airship?

Airships come in three types: rigid, with light-alloy framework hulls; nonrigid, with no framework; and a combination of both. Rigid airships, like the ill-fated *Hindenburg*, have disappeared, and nonrigid types—blimps—are today's norm.

Blimps consist of a large, helium-filled polyester envelope, with a gondola suspended below. Within the envelope is a two-part bag called the ballonet. Shifting the air within the ballonet raises or lowers the blimp's nose. Propeller motors on the gondola move the blimp forward, while four stabilizers adjust course and altitude.

Ground ropes

Exhaust and intake port

Airships are an impressive sight, attracting attention that makes them a popular medium for aerial advertising displays.

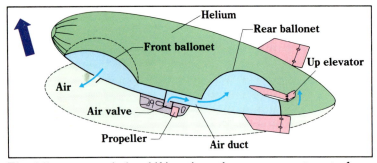

The blimp ascends by shifting air to the rear compartment of the ballonet, tilting the nose upward.

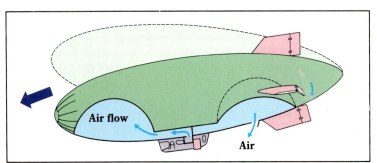

The blimp descends when air shifts to the forward part of the ballonet, tilting the nose downward.

The ballonet

Because helium is lighter than air, the more air that enters the ballonet, the heavier it becomes. Air can be shifted between the forward and aft compartments of the ballonet to increase the weight of the nose or tail. As air fills the aft compartment, the tail of the airship sinks, causing the nose to rise. Using this ballast along with engine thrust and elevator control, the pilot can cause the airship to ascend or descend.

Propellers

The pilot controls ascent and descent by shifting air in the ballonet and also by changing the angle of the propeller motors, pulling the airship either upward or downward.

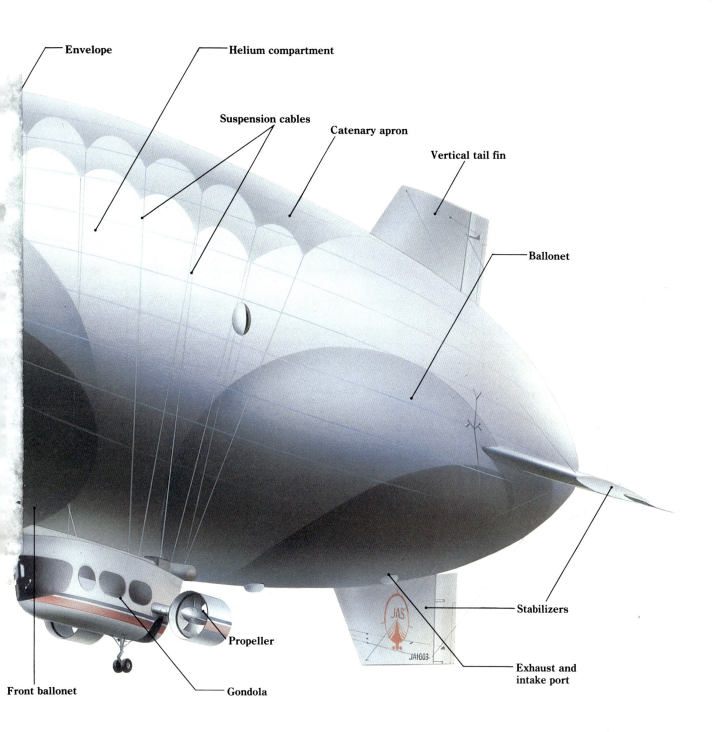

Envelope

Helium compartment

Suspension cables

Catenary apron

Vertical tail fin

Ballonet

Stabilizers

Exhaust and intake port

Propeller

Gondola

Front ballonet

Turning left and right

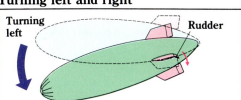

Turning left

Rudder

Turning the vertical tail fin rudders to the left causes the airship to turn left.

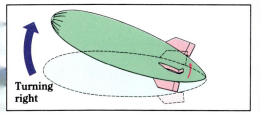

Turning right

Turning the vertical tail fin rudders to the right causes the airship to turn right.

Construction of the gondola

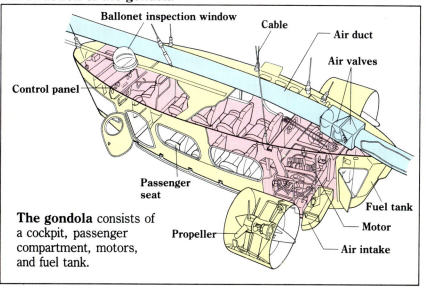

Ballonet inspection window

Cable

Air duct

Air valves

Control panel

Passenger seat

Propeller

Fuel tank

Motor

Air intake

The gondola consists of a cockpit, passenger compartment, motors, and fuel tank.

How Do Gliders Stay Up?

A soaring glider relies on the same lift force that allows ordinary planes to fly. In powered flight, lift is generated over the wings as the engine propels the plane through the air. Gliders use gravity as their source of power, rather than an engine. The glider's forward airspeed—provided by the initial takeoff tow and by the pull of gravity and thermal updrafts—provides a swift flow of air over and under the wings, generating lift.

A slender, soaring glider has a narrow fuselage and long wings for greater lift than powered craft.

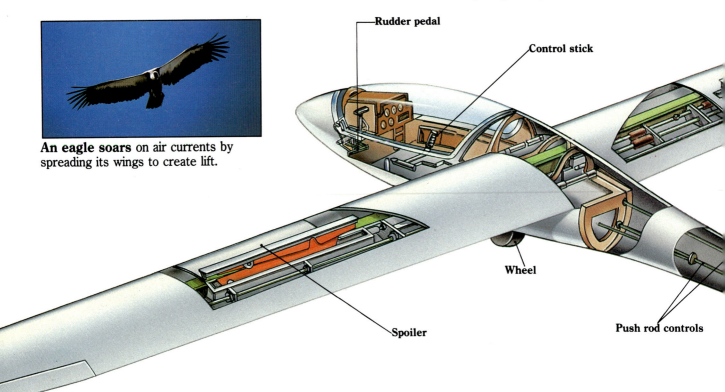

An eagle soars on air currents by spreading its wings to create lift.

Rudder pedal

Control stick

Wheel

Push rod controls

Spoiler

The principle of soaring

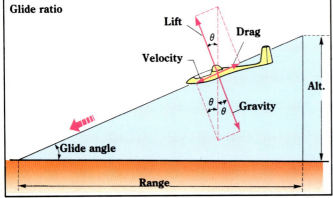

Glide ratio

Lift

Drag

Velocity

θ

Gravity

θ θ

Alt.

Glide angle

Range

A glider pilot must balance the four forces of gravity, lift, drag, and velocity.

Function of the spoiler

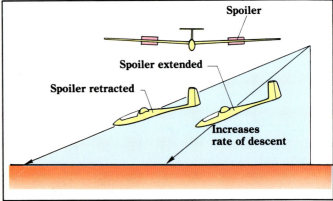

Spoiler

Spoiler extended

Spoiler retracted

Increases rate of descent

Gliders fly by maintaining an optimum angle relative to the ground. To land, spoilers on the wing are raised to create air resistance and alter the speed and approach angle.

Getting aloft

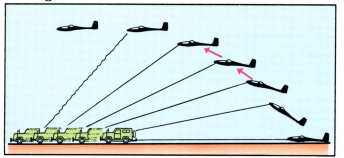

A glider may be towed into the sky by a car or a power winch on the ground.

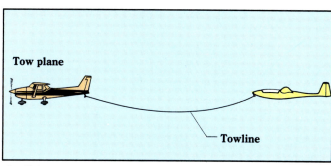

A glider may also be pulled aloft by a tow plane, which then releases the glider to fly on its own.

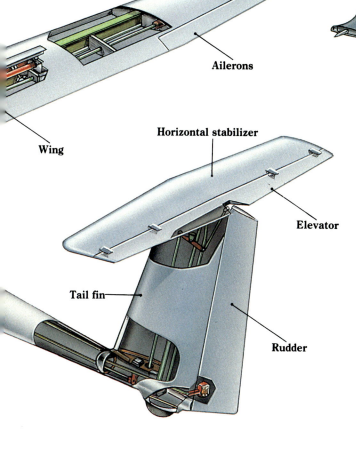

Ailerons

Wing

Horizontal stabilizer

Elevator

Tail fin

Rudder

Riding the air currents

A glider's time in the air can be considerably extended by a pilot who makes skillful use of the prevailing air currents.

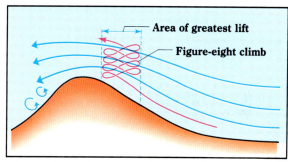

Area of greatest lift

Figure-eight climb

Mountain updrafts provide tremendous lift, as strong winds meet and flow upslope.

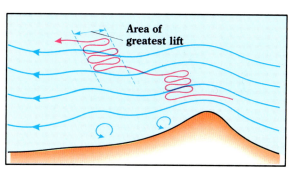

Area of greatest lift

Winds striking a peak create mountain-wave updrafts above the opposite slope.

A glider deploys its spoilers to adjust its speed.

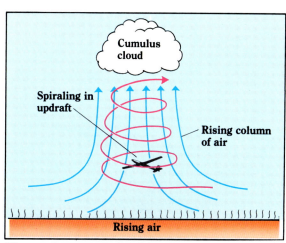

Cumulus cloud

Spiraling in updraft

Rising column of air

Rising air

Thermals, or updrafts rising from sun-warmed ground, can carry gliders to great altitudes.

How Is Air Traffic Controlled?

Every day, thousands of aircraft crowd the skies. To ensure safety and efficiency, international flight rules governing all air traffic have been established. Planes follow flight corridors about 9 miles wide, separated by a vertical difference of 1,000 to 2,000 feet. Aircraft heading in compass directions from 0 to 179 degrees fly at altitudes of odd-numbered thousand-foot increments, such as 3,000 feet and 5,000 feet. Aircraft bound in directions from 180 to 359 degrees fly at even-numbered altitudes. In this way, aircraft approaching one another are separated by at least 1,000 feet. Above 29,000 feet, planes maintain intervals of at least 2,000 feet. Small private aircraft have no fixed routes and may choose their own flight plans as long as they obey local rules.

Instrument flight

Aircraft on instrument-controlled flights fly safely by maintaining established distances from other airborne traffic. Cruising altitudes are determined for every flight direction, and aircraft maintain vertical intervals of at least 1,000 feet.

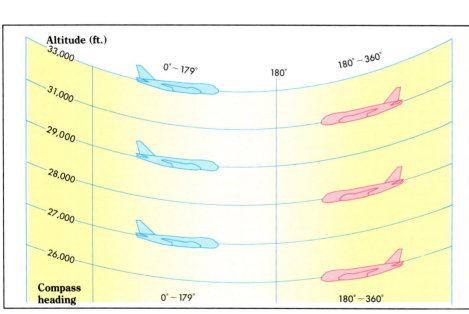

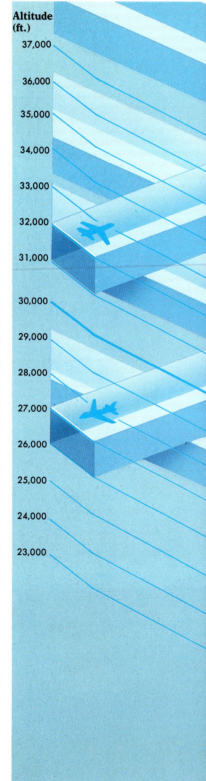

Landing safely

In this diagram, distance between cruising flights is maintained in 10-minute intervals.

An approaching flight descends with a five-minute interval between it and other traffic.

An ascending plane also keeps a five-minute interval separating it from other planes.

Transatlantic flight corridors

On flights from London to New York, passenger planes crossing the Atlantic fly at a cruising altitude of about 35,000 feet. After takeoff, planes maintain a steady ascent for about 300 miles before leveling off at their cruising altitude. Because of strong westerly winds on this route, it takes longer to fly from London to New York than from New York to London.

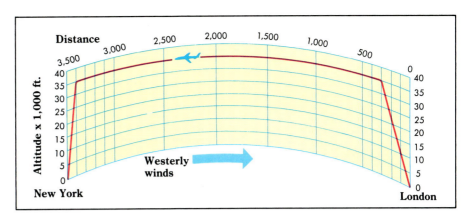

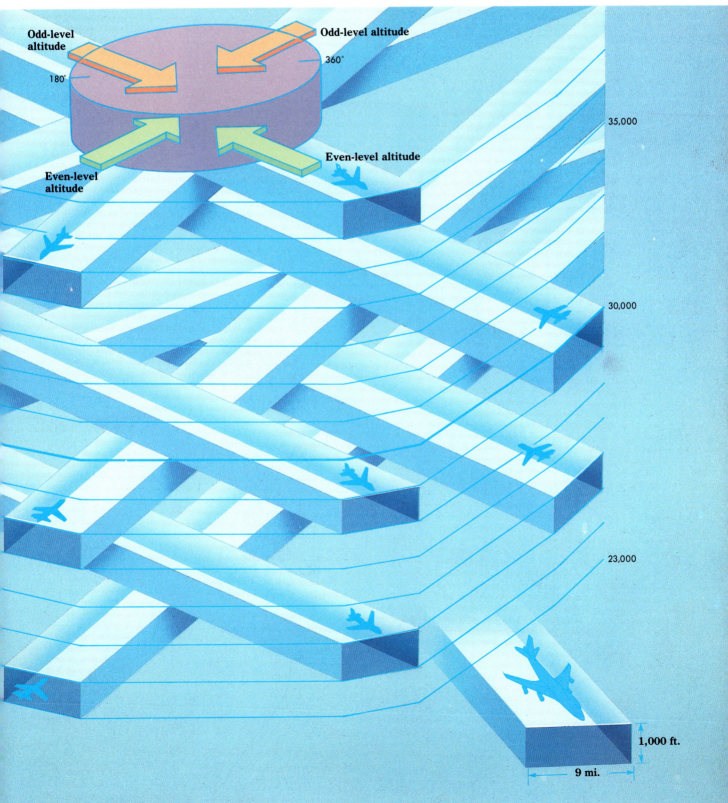

How Do Pilots Follow Air Routes?

Large passenger planes such as the Boeing 747 jumbo jet follow traffic corridors that spread in all directions and are connected by ground-based navigational aids called VOR (very high frequency Omnirange). A VOR station emits two radio waves that show both magnetic north and every direction throughout 360 degrees. The flight navigator reads the radio waves over a VOR receiver and finds the plane's direction and location relative to the VOR station. Correct headings are indicated on the RMI (radio magnetic indicator), the HSI (horizontal situation indicator), and the CDI (course deviation indicator).

A VOR station emits a radio wave that navigators use to find their positions.

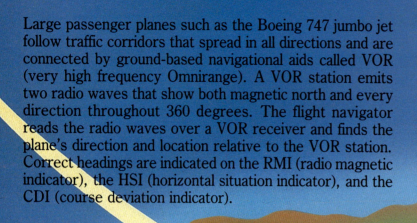

VOR

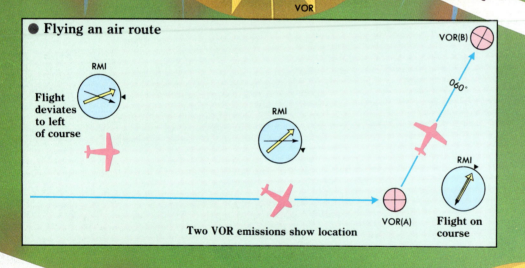

● **Flying an air route**

RMI

Flight deviates to left of course

RMI

VOR(B)

060°

RMI

VOR(A)

Flight on course

Two VOR emissions show location

VOR

VOR

VOR

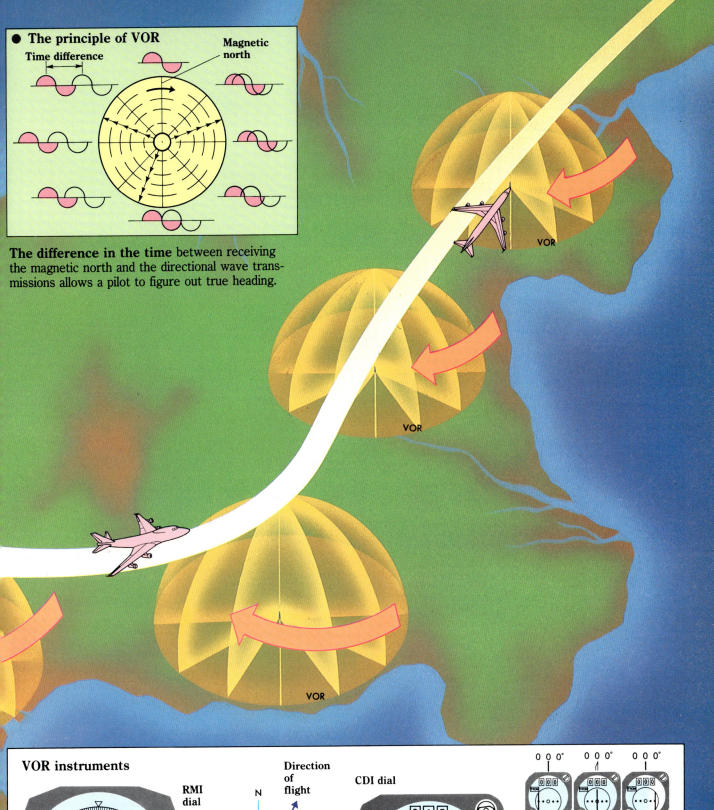

● The principle of VOR

Time difference

Magnetic north

The difference in the time between receiving the magnetic north and the directional wave transmissions allows a pilot to figure out true heading.

VOR

VOR

VOR

VOR instruments

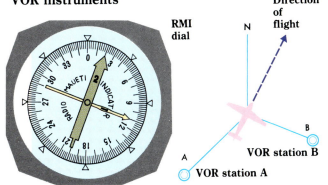

RMI dial

Direction of flight

N

VOR station B

A

VOR station A

Needles indicate the directions of VOR stations. In the diagram above, the thin needle gives the heading of VOR station A, the broad needle, VOR B.

CDI dial

015

TO

MARKER

SET

The position of the needle gives plane's location relative to the VOR station.

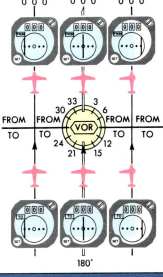

0 0 0°   0 0 0°   0 0 0°

FROM FROM   FROM FROM
TO   TO   TO   TO

33 3
30   6
VOR
24   12
21 15

180°

Why Don't Aircraft Get Lost?

When aircraft fly over areas where there are no ground radio guidance stations, such as over the ocean, pilots can find out where they are by using an INS, or inertial navigation system. The INS, which consists of a gyroscope and built-in accelerometers, helps calculate the direction of flight, speed, and distance traveled. The gyroscope helps to keep the aircraft level at a right angle to the downward pull of gravity. The accelerometers, located in the horizontal stabilizer, detect the acceleration of the airplane in any direction, and a computer uses the data to calculate the motion and location of the aircraft.

The INS is connected to the autopilot in the cockpit. Before takeoff, the pilot enters the desired flight plan, course settings, speed, and altitude in the computer. Using this information, the computer then directs the flight to its destination, following the predetermined course, without any additional support from the ground.

INS (inertial navigation system)

The horizontal stabilizer contains two accelerometers. The X-accelerometer detects acceleration in the east and west directions, while the Y-accelerometer detects south and north acceleration. An aircraft is constantly accelerating as it flies. Data that record this motion are used to calculate the speed of the plane and the distance it has traveled.

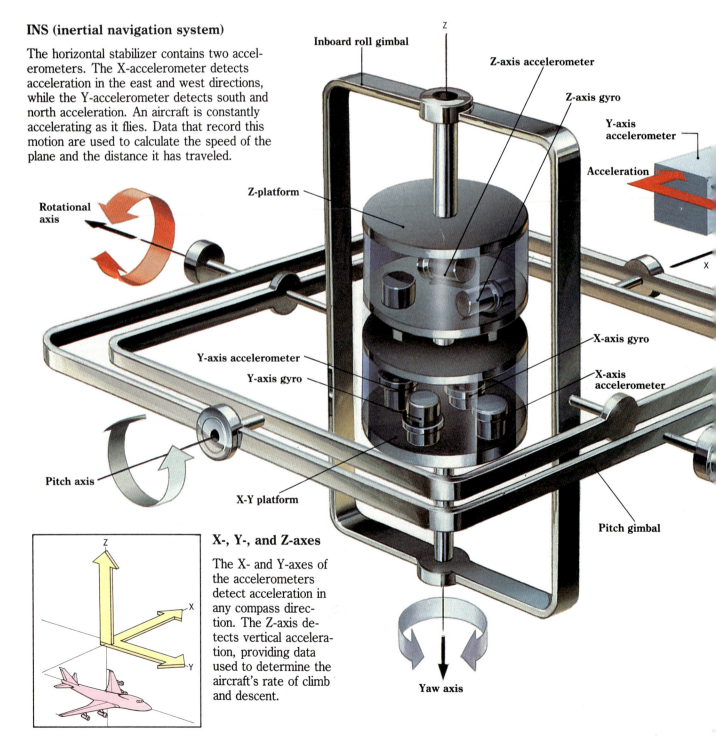

Inboard roll gimbal

Z-axis accelerometer

Z-axis gyro

Y-axis accelerometer

Acceleration

Z-platform

Rotational axis

X-axis gyro

Y-axis accelerometer

Y-axis gyro

X-axis accelerometer

Pitch axis

X-Y platform

Pitch gimbal

Yaw axis

X-, Y-, and Z-axes

The X- and Y-axes of the accelerometers detect acceleration in any compass direction. The Z-axis detects vertical acceleration, providing data used to determine the aircraft's rate of climb and descent.

The Omega System

The Omega System determines aircraft location by calculating the difference in time of the reception of radio waves broadcast from two ground stations. Using a very low frequency (VLF) of 10 to 14 kHz, the Omega System covers the entire Earth's surface from a network of just eight stations. With this system, a navigator can find his or her own plane at any point in the sky throughout the world. The Omega stations are located in North Dakota, Hawaii, Norway, Liberia, Argentina, Australia, Japan, and Réunion Island in the Indian Ocean.

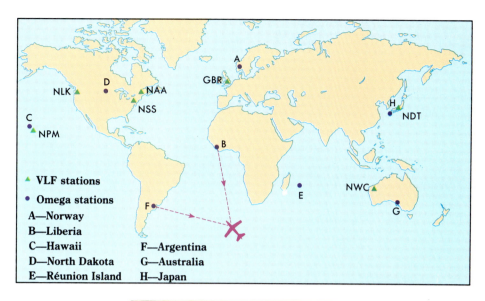

▲ VLF stations
● Omega stations
A—Norway
B—Liberia
C—Hawaii
D—North Dakota
E—Réunion Island
F—Argentina
G—Australia
H—Japan

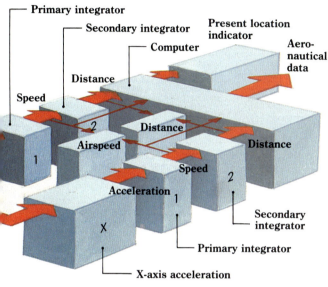

Primary integrator
Secondary integrator
Computer
Present location indicator
Aeronautical data
Distance
Speed
Distance
Airspeed
Distance
Speed
Acceleration
Secondary integrator
Primary integrator
X-axis acceleration
Outboard roll gimbal

The cockpit INS system looks complicated but is actually quite simple to operate. The pilot enters the flight plan on the keypad, and after a pause, the mode selector lamp turns green, indicating that the computer has accepted the data.

Putting it together

The flight plan entered in the INS includes the latitude and longitude of the destination and landmarks en route. The computer processes this information together with data from the accelerometers to calculate the aircraft's speed and distance traveled. Cockpit instruments also display the plane's air- and ground-speed, present position, heading, and wind direction and velocity.

An INS-equipped aircraft can plot its location anywhere in the world.

How Do Airplanes Land in Fog?

Instrument landing system (ILS)

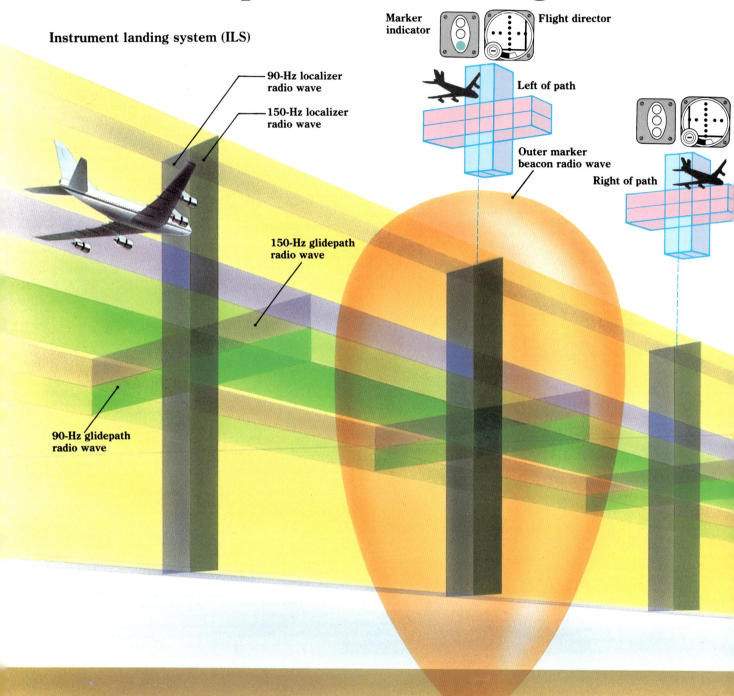

Marker indicator

Flight director

90-Hz localizer radio wave

150-Hz localizer radio wave

Left of path

Outer marker beacon radio wave

Right of path

150-Hz glidepath radio wave

90-Hz glidepath radio wave

Outer marker beacon

Airplanes can land safely in every kind of weather thanks to the instrument landing system, or ILS. When visibility is poor, pilots rely both on information from the instruments in the plane's cockpit and on directional guidance signals sent from the airport's ILS, which consists of a localizer, a glidepath indicator, and a series of consecutive markers. The localizer indicates variations in the plane's position to the left or right of the runway's centerline, the glidepath indicator moni-

tors the plane's angle of descent, and the markers give the distance from the runway. By using the ILS, pilots can maintain the correct course and attitude even when visibility is zero.

At many airports, ILS is now being replaced by the improved microwave landing system (MLS), which uses two ground-based microwave transmitters. This creates an expanded instrument landing system that can handle more aircraft in greater safety than the ILS.

The cockpit instrument panel includes ILS equipment and the flight director.

Instrument landing system

The ILS localizer broadcasts two radio waves at 90-Hz FM and 150-Hz FM. The 90-Hz signal dominates the zone to the left of the glidepath, and the 150-Hz signal dominates the zone to the right *(below)*. The strength of each signal lets the pilot know whether the plane is left or right of the centerline, where the two signals are of equal strength. Similarly, two signals monitor rate of descent along the glidepath. If the plane is above the ideal 2.5- to 3-degree angle of descent toward the runway, the 150-Hz signal dominates, while the 90-Hz signal dominates the lower angles. Three marker beacons placed along the approach to the runway transmit directional signals at 400, 1,300, and 3,000 Hz showing distance from the runway, ranging from about ½ mile to about 5 miles.

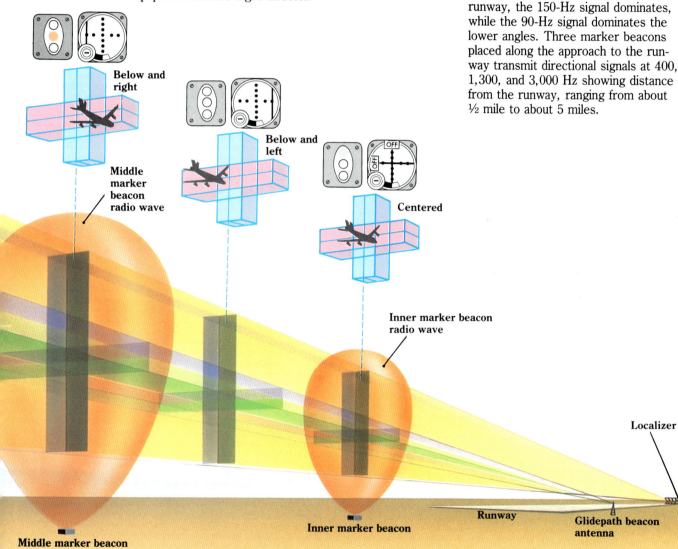

Below and right

Middle marker beacon radio wave

Below and left

Centered

Inner marker beacon radio wave

Localizer

Inner marker beacon

Runway

Glidepath beacon antenna

Middle marker beacon

● ILS indicator

The ILS indicator in the cockpit receives signals from the localizer, glide-path, and location markers. These data are sent to the flight director, at the upper left of the photo. Lights at the upper right of the photo flash on and off as the aircraft passes each marker.

● Flight director (FD)

The flight director tells the pilot where he or she is in relation to the glidepath. The pilot guides the plane by making constant adjustments in order to keep the vertical and horizontal bars on the FD crossed at right angles in the center of the instrument.

How Are Aircraft Pressurized?

As an airplane climbs higher into the sky, atmospheric pressure outside the plane drops. Therefore, a plane must have a special air-conditioning system to pump air into the cabin and keep the air pressure safe and comfortable for the passengers. To do this, outside air is pumped into the cabin from the engines and controlled through a series of pressure-control valves. At the same time, impure air from inside the cabin must be vented to the outside. In most passenger aircraft, pressure is maintained at one atmosphere (that is, equal to the pressure at sea level) up to 22,500 feet, and at 80 percent of sea-level pressure up to 36,000 feet.

Air circulation in an airplane

After adjustments are made in pressure and temperature, air taken in by the engines is pumped into the cabin and cockpit via special ventilation ducts.

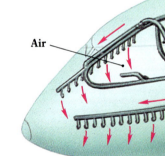

Wing

Air

Engines

Air

Air

Air-conditioning units

Air

Pumping air into the airplane

The air-conditioning unit sends air from the engines into the cabin through ducts in the ceiling. Air circulates throughout the cabin and then is vented out the rear through pressure control valves.

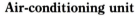

Into the airplane

From right engines

From left engines

Air-conditioning unit

Air-conditioning unit

The air-conditioning unit is located in the center of the aircraft. It combines an air circulator and a heat exchanger to cool air from the engines before it passes into the cabin.

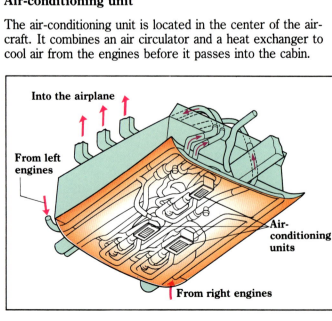

Into the airplane

From left engines

Air-conditioning units

From right engines

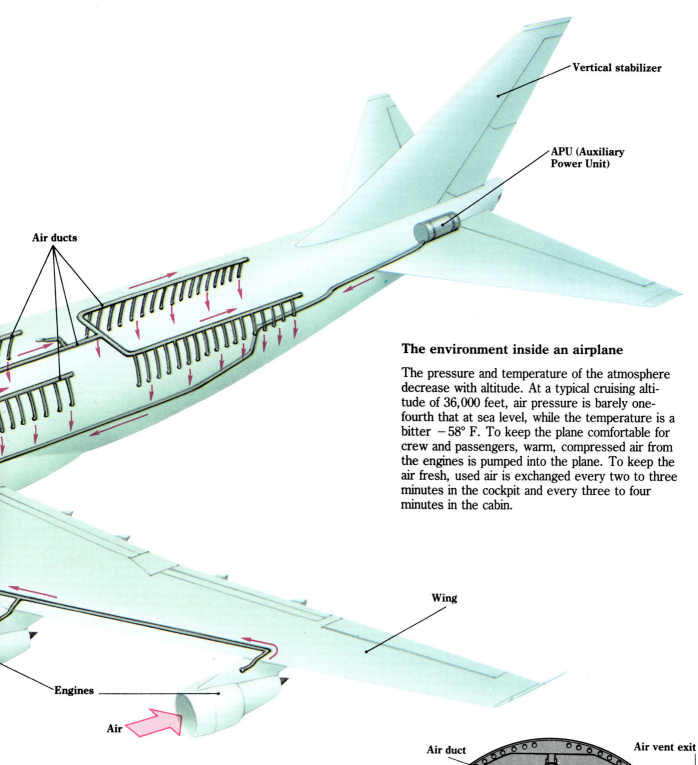

Air ducts

Vertical stabilizer

APU (Auxiliary
Power Unit)

The environment inside an airplane

The pressure and temperature of the atmosphere decrease with altitude. At a typical cruising altitude of 36,000 feet, air pressure is barely one-fourth that at sea level, while the temperature is a bitter −58° F. To keep the plane comfortable for crew and passengers, warm, compressed air from the engines is pumped into the plane. To keep the air fresh, used air is exchanged every two to three minutes in the cockpit and every three to four minutes in the cabin.

Wing

Engines

Air

Engine air intake mechanism

This mechanism cools and purifies hot, high-pressure compressed air from the engines before introducing it into the cabin.

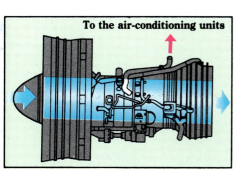

To the air-conditioning units

Air circulation

Air circulates from ceiling ducts, through the cabin, then under the floor and back to release vents.

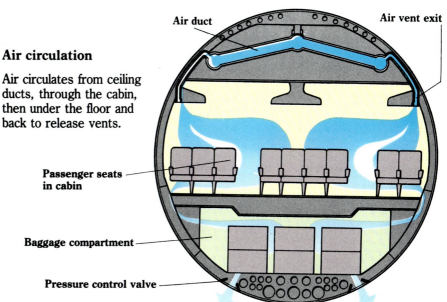

Air duct

Air vent exit

Passenger seats
in cabin

Baggage compartment

Pressure control valve

How Does a Jet Engine Work?

A propeller pulls an aircraft forward, but a jet engine pushes it ahead with the thrust created by expelling hot exhaust gases to the rear at a high velocity. There are four types of jet, or turbine, engines: turbojets; turbofans, such as those used on passenger jets like the Boeing 747; turboprops, which employ turbine-powered propellers; and turboshafts, used in helicopters.

A turbofan engine consists of three components: a compressor, a combustor, and a turbine to produce power. First, air is taken into the engine and compressed by a rotational fan. In the combustor, the compressed air combines with fuel and ignites, producing a high-temperature, high-pressure gas. This gas passes through the turbine, causing it to rotate at a high speed. Thrust is created when the gas is forced out the rear of the engine as exhaust.

Mechanism of a turbofan engine

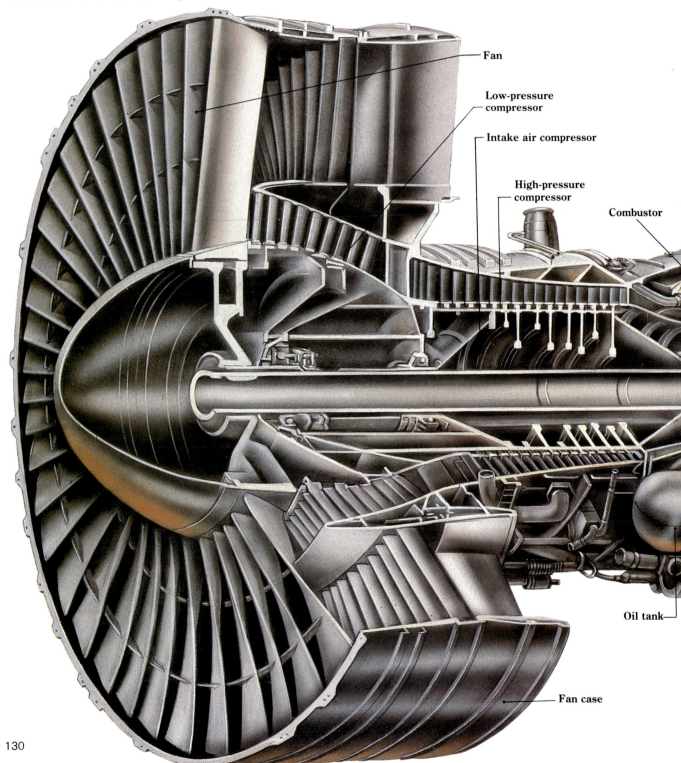

Fan

Low-pressure compressor

Intake air compressor

High-pressure compressor

Combustor

Oil tank

Fan case

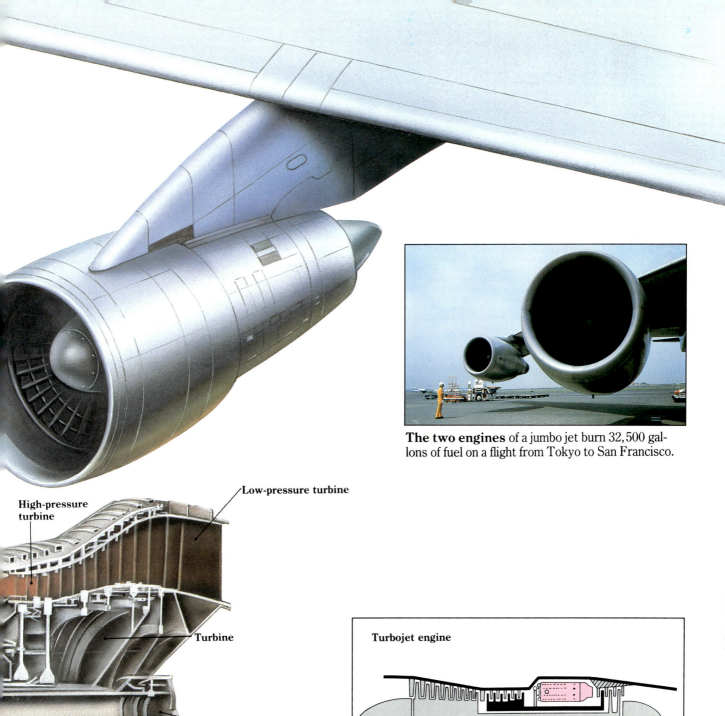

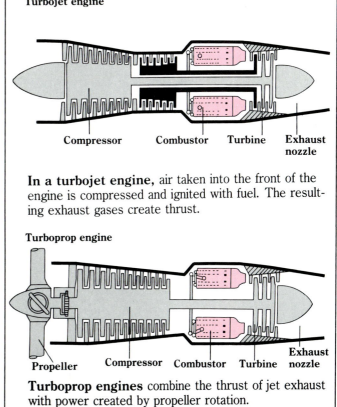

The two engines of a jumbo jet burn 32,500 gallons of fuel on a flight from Tokyo to San Francisco.

High-pressure turbine

Low-pressure turbine

Turbine

Rotor shaft

After a turbine engine pulls in air, the gas pressure is raised through a series of compression stages. Both the pressure and volume grow significantly when ignition occurs in the combustor. The thrust created by the exhaust allows jet-powered aircraft to reach much higher speeds and altitudes than are possible for piston-driven propeller aircraft.

Turbojet engine

Compressor   Combustor   Turbine   Exhaust nozzle

In a turbojet engine, air taken into the front of the engine is compressed and ignited with fuel. The resulting exhaust gases create thrust.

Turboprop engine

Propeller   Compressor   Combustor   Turbine   Exhaust nozzle

Turboprop engines combine the thrust of jet exhaust with power created by propeller rotation.

How Are Height and Speed Measured?

The speed and altitude of an airplane are measured by instruments called airspeed indicators and altimeters. Speed is determined by measuring pressure differences in the air passing through a tube, called a Pitot tube, located in the wing or nose. An aneroid barometer senses the pressure differences and expands or contracts in response. These motions of the barometer move an indicator, which controls a gauge on the cockpit instrument panel. The faster the plane moves, the greater the difference in air pressure at the two ends of the Pitot tube.

Altitude is measured in two ways. An atmospheric pressure altimeter simply measures the changing pressure outside the plane as it climbs or descends. The vacuum aneroid is affected by pressure changes, and the varying tension on a spring in the aneroid is translated into altimeter readings. A radio wave altimeter measures altitude as a function of the time it takes for radio waves sent by the plane to reflect off the ground and return to the plane.

Mach airspeed indicator

The mach indicator measures airspeed relative to the speed of sound, known as mach 1. Differences in pressure are measured between the tip of the Pitot tube and the stationary pressure nozzle on its side. Two aneroid barometers shrink or expand as a function of air pressure, and these motions are reflected on the airspeed indicator.

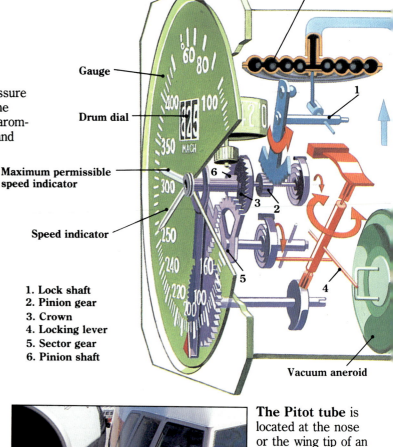

Aneroid pressure differential

Gauge

Drum dial

Maximum permissible speed indicator

Speed indicator

1. Lock shaft
2. Pinion gear
3. Crown
4. Locking lever
5. Sector gear
6. Pinion shaft

Vacuum aneroid

Anatomy of the Pitot tube

The Pitot tube measures both the pressure of the oncoming airflow and the static pressure along the sides of the tube. The difference in the two readings tells the pilot the airspeed.

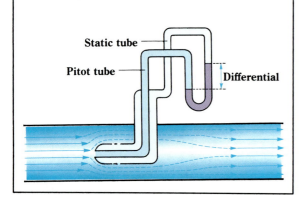

Static tube

Pitot tube

Differential

The Pitot tube is located at the nose or the wing tip of an aircraft.

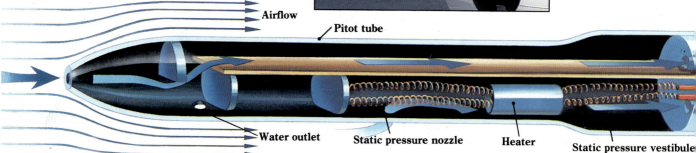

Airflow

Pitot tube

Water outlet

Static pressure nozzle

Heater

Static pressure vestibule

The mach indicator is named after physicist Ernst Mach, who studied the speed of sound— about 760 mph at sea level.

Altimeter

An atmospheric pressure altimeter uses a barometer to measure changes in air pressure outside the plane as it moves up or down. Altitude in feet or meters is shown on the cockpit instrument panel. Pressure altimeters must be adjusted to allow for changes in atmospheric pressure due to variable weather conditions.

Aneroid altimeter

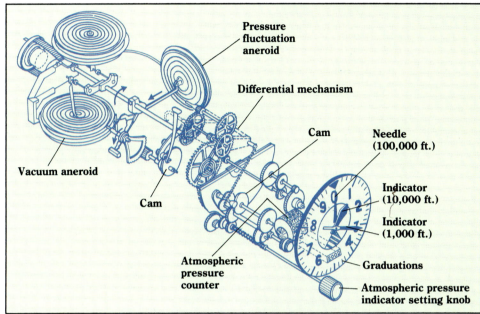

Radio altimeter

There are two types of radio altimeter. One finds altitude from the difference in frequencies of radio waves sent to the ground and reflected back to the plane *(right)*. The other type measures the time interval between the transmission and the return of the signals. The first type is used mainly for low-altitude measurements; the second type, for high-altitude measurements.

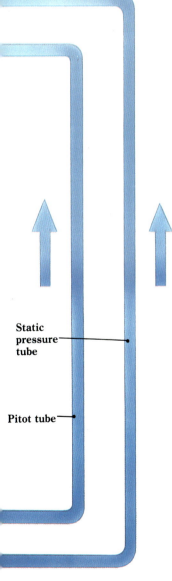

Static pressure tube

Pitot tube

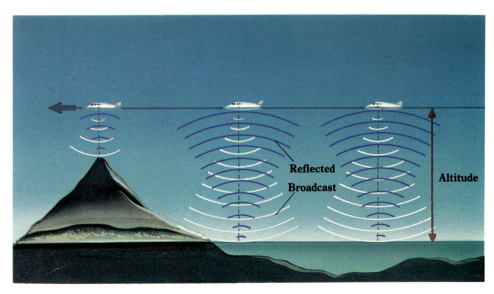

What Was the First Airplane?

Orville and Wilbur Wright, two brothers from Dayton, Ohio, achieved the first successful flight of a powered, heavier-than-air vehicle at Kill Devil Hills, North Carolina, on December 17, 1903. Their first flight, with Orville as the pilot, lasted just 12 seconds and covered only 120 feet.

With a wingspan of 40 feet, the Wright *Flyer* was powered by a lightweight four-cylinder gasoline engine that generated 12 horsepower and spun the plane's propellers via a chain drive. The *Flyer* featured flexible wing tips that could be bent to steer the plane.

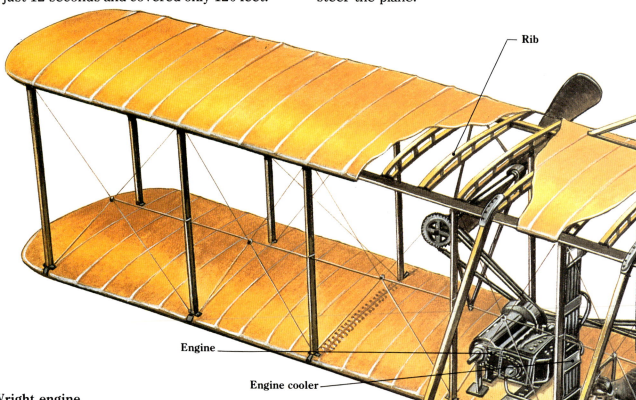

Rib

Engine

Engine cooler

Landing skids

Elevators

The Wright engine

Bicycle builders by trade, the Wright brothers saw a significant advance with their development of a lightweight gasoline engine. The chain transmission spun the propellers in opposite directions.

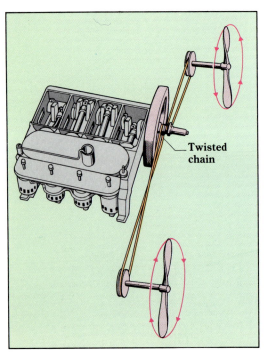

Twisted chain

The Wright propellers

The Wright *Flyer*'s propellers were made of spruce and had an aerodynamic cross section similar to that of the wing. They could transfer about 65 percent of the engine's power into propulsion. The best modern propellers achieve about 85 percent efficiency.

Piloting the *Flyer*

Observing that birds controlled their flight by twisting their wing tips, the Wrights emulated nature in their *Flyer*. A hip cradle moved from side to side to twist the wing tips in opposite directions for lateral control. A control stick governed climb and descent.

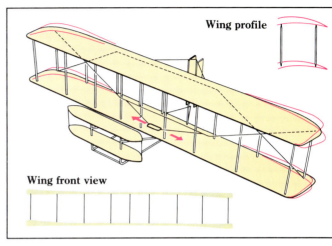

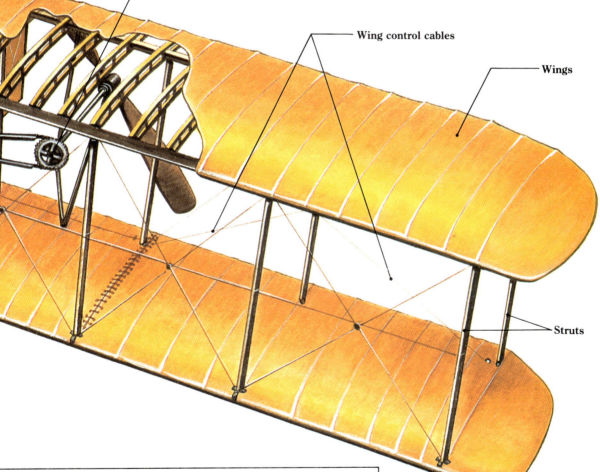

An ancient dream was realized as the *Flyer* took to the air.

Rudder

Propellers

Transmission gear

Wing control cables

Wings

Struts

Wing profile

Wing front view

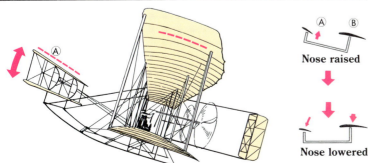

Nose raised

Nose lowered

The Wright control system

Climb and descent were controlled by twin elevators mounted in front of the wings. This structure, known as a canard, kept the aircraft stable at low speeds. Unlike in a conventional airplane, with elevators in the rear, if the *Flyer*'s nose rose too high, the elevators stalled before the wings and gently dipped downward to restore equilibrium to the craft.

What Is Supersonic Flight?

The sound barrier was first broken in 1947 by test pilot Charles Yeager in the experimental Bell X-1. Today, the Anglo-French Concorde routinely flies at supersonic speeds. The speed of sound, which varies with atmospheric pressure and temperature, is 760 mph at sea level but about 660 mph at 40,000 feet. As an airplane approaches the speed of sound, air pressure builds up in front of the craft, creating a "barrier." Exceeding this speed creates a shock wave (or sonic boom) which can cause a pilot to lose control of the plane. Supersonic craft like the Concorde are designed to withstand such stress.

The Concorde takes to the air, its nose tilted downward.

Wing and fuselage design

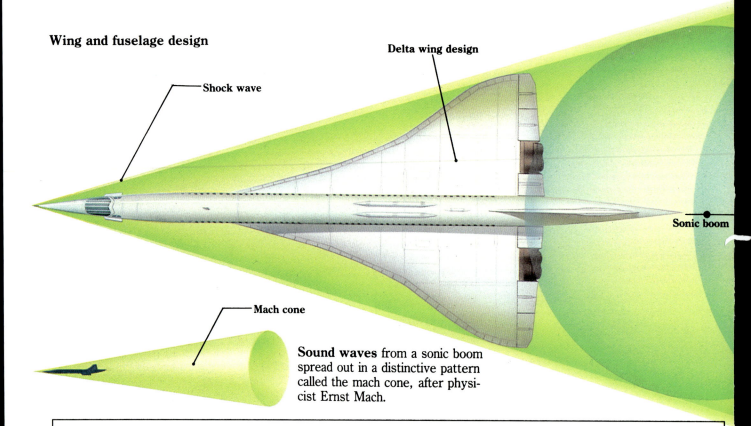

Delta wing design

Shock wave

Sonic boom

Mach cone

Sound waves from a sonic boom spread out in a distinctive pattern called the mach cone, after physicist Ernst Mach.

Speed and shock waves

1. At subsonic speeds, a plane's sound wave passes through the air in front of the aircraft.

2. Air pressure and sound waves build up ahead of the aircraft as it approaches the speed of sound.

3. At supersonic speeds, a conic shock wave extends backward along the edges of the sound wave.

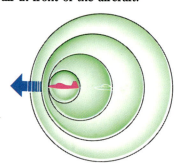
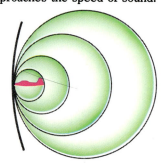
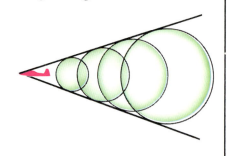

An adjustable nose

The Concorde has a unique nose, which tilts downward to provide the pilot with greater visibility for takeoffs and landings. At cruising speed, the nose is raised to reduce air resistance.

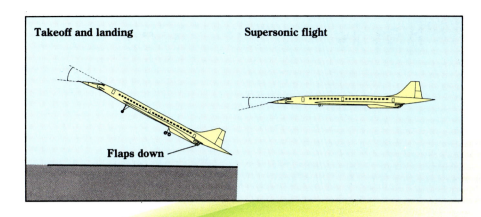

Takeoff and landing   Supersonic flight

Flaps down

Mach cone

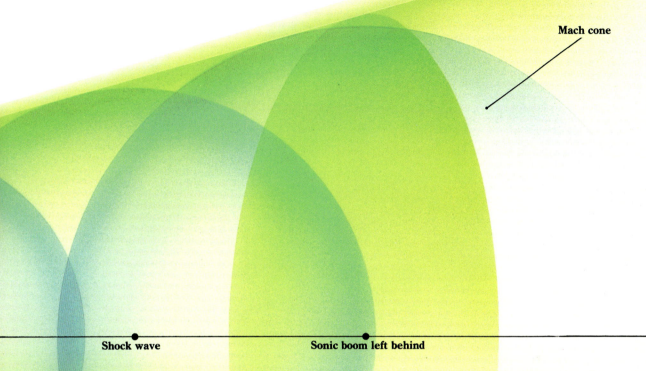

Shock wave   Sonic boom left behind

Supersonic aircraft like the Concorde rely on powerful engines and a sleek, aerodynamic design to achieve supersonic speeds. The design must be capable of withstanding the turbulence created when breaking the sound barrier. The Concorde's smoothly swept delta wings enable it to remain stable both at supersonic speeds and at low speeds as well. Because the sonic boom can cause damage on the ground, the Concorde remains at subsonic speeds when flying over land.

What Is a VTOL Aircraft?

Most aircraft need long runways on which to gain speed for takeoff or to slow down after landing. But VTOL (vertical takeoff and landing) aircraft, such as the Harrier fighter, can take off and land almost anywhere. Four movable jet exhausts can aim the engine's thrust in varying directions. By changing the direction of these nozzles, the plane can take off or land vertically, or fly forward like a normal jet.

The Harrier "jump jet" fighter

The Harrier's jet exhausts can move.

Wing

Forward jet exhaust

Intake

Pitot tube

Nose landing gear bay

Aerial cannons

Vertical takeoff maneuver

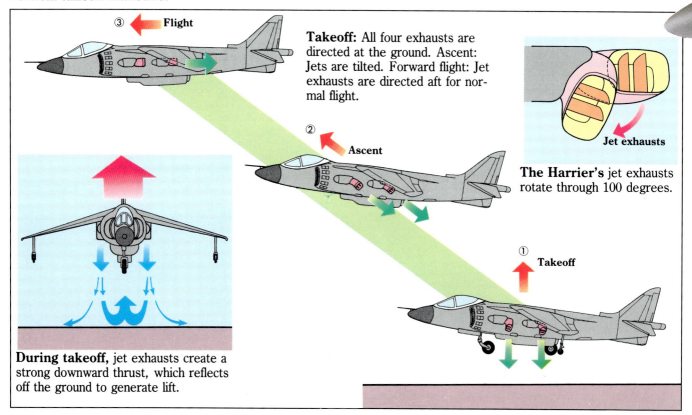

③ Flight

Takeoff: All four exhausts are directed at the ground. Ascent: Jets are tilted. Forward flight: Jet exhausts are directed aft for normal flight.

② Ascent

Jet exhausts

The Harrier's jet exhausts rotate through 100 degrees.

① Takeoff

During takeoff, jet exhausts create a strong downward thrust, which reflects off the ground to generate lift.

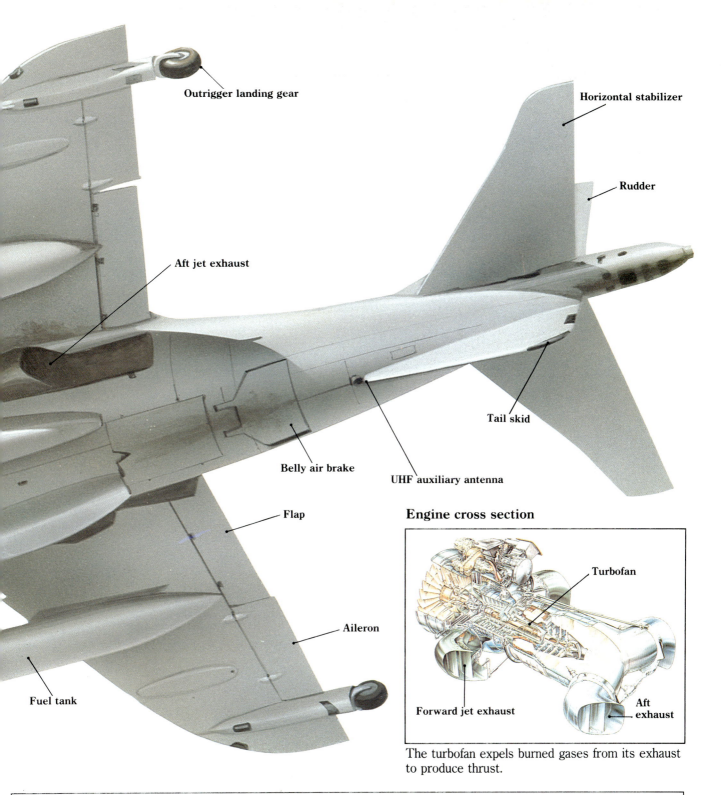

Outrigger landing gear

Horizontal stabilizer

Rudder

Aft jet exhaust

Tail skid

Belly air brake

UHF auxiliary antenna

Flap

Aileron

Fuel tank

Engine cross section

Turbofan

Forward jet exhaust

Aft exhaust

The turbofan expels burned gases from its exhaust to produce thrust.

Other VTOL aircraft

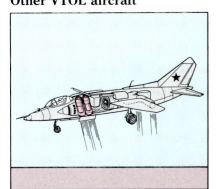

The Forger has two special engines for VTOL maneuvers, as well as a flight engine.

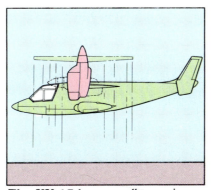

The XV-15 has propeller engines mounted on the wings, which rotate upward for VTOL.

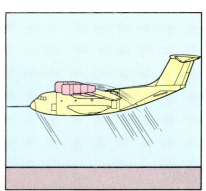

The Asuka STOL (short takeoff and landing) has exhausts that point downward for quick takeoffs.

How Do Some Aircraft Fly Sideways?

Normally, an airplane flies only in the direction its nose is pointed, but some military aircraft can almost dance in the sky. The CCV (Control-Configured Vehicle), a jet fighter, can fly not only forward, but up, down, and sideways as well. Sideways flight is made possible by small, movable wings, called canards, located forward of the aircraft's main wings. During up-and-down flight, the angles of the horizontal canards and the horizontal stabilizers are adjusted, while similar adjustments are made to the vertical canard and the

rudder for sideways flight. This innovative design makes it possible for the CCV to change direction or altitude while staying horizontal, through a combination of adjustments to the horizontal canards, the vertical canard, the leading edge flaps, the horizontal stabilizers, the rudder, and the trailing edge flaps.

The CCV

Pitot tube

Vertical canard

The vertical canard

For sudden maneuvers during straight flight, the vertical canard (forward of and below the wings) is adjusted sideways along with the rudder. The plane then moves sideways, while the nose continues to point forward.

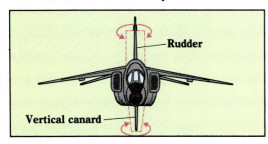

Rudder

Vertical canard

Conventional plane

CCV

Horizontal CCV attack maneuver

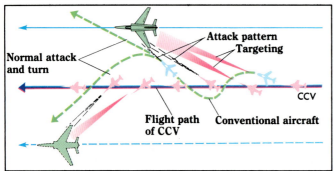

Attack pattern
Targeting
Normal attack and turn
CCV
Flight path of CCV
Conventional aircraft

The CCV's ability to suddenly change direction eliminates the need for long, complicated S-curve maneuvers.

Ground attack capability

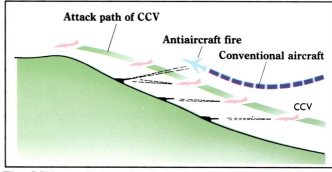

Attack path of CCV
Antiaircraft fire
Conventional aircraft
CCV

The CCV can climb while aiming its nose at the ground, avoiding the need for circling the ground target.

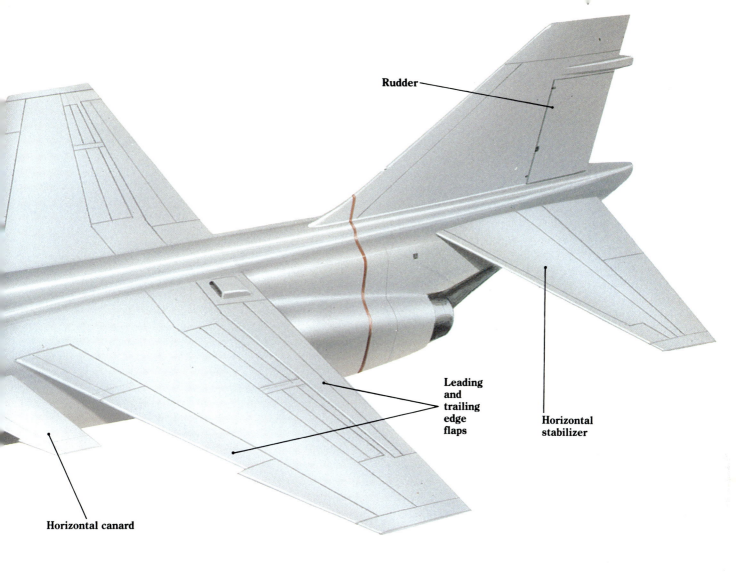

Rudder

Leading
and
trailing
edge
flaps

Horizontal
stabilizer

Horizontal canard

The horizontal canard

For sudden up-and-down movements, the horizontal canard and the horizontal stabilizer are raised or lowered, lifting or dropping the craft while maintaining its nose-forward attitude.

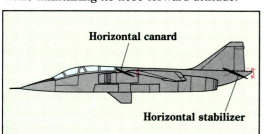

Horizontal canard

Horizontal stabilizer

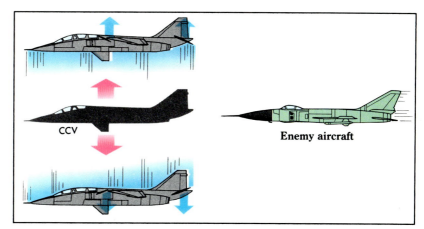

CCV

Enemy aircraft

Loop maneuvers

Conventional fighters require a lot of room when performing loops to escape pursuing enemy planes. The CCV, in contrast, can adjust its vertical canard and horizontal stabilizer to perform short loops that are impossible for conventional planes. Though it is less stable in ordinary flight than a conventional plane, its unique capabilities can give the CCV a decisive advantage in a dogfight.

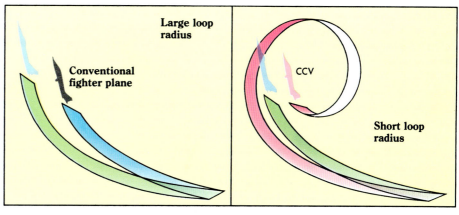

Large loop
radius

Conventional
fighter plane

CCV

Short loop
radius

What Is a Forward-Swept Wing?

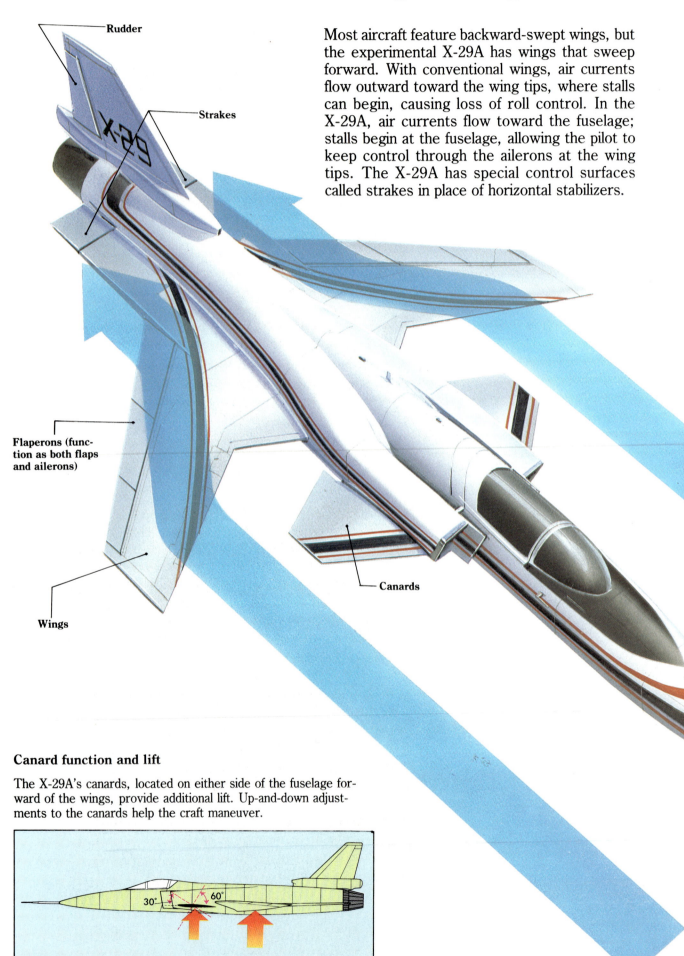

Rudder

Strakes

Flaperons (function as both flaps and ailerons)

Wings

Canards

Most aircraft feature backward-swept wings, but the experimental X-29A has wings that sweep forward. With conventional wings, air currents flow outward toward the wing tips, where stalls can begin, causing loss of roll control. In the X-29A, air currents flow toward the fuselage; stalls begin at the fuselage, allowing the pilot to keep control through the ailerons at the wing tips. The X-29A has special control surfaces called strakes in place of horizontal stabilizers.

Canard function and lift

The X-29A's canards, located on either side of the fuselage forward of the wings, provide additional lift. Up-and-down adjustments to the canards help the craft maneuver.

30° 60°

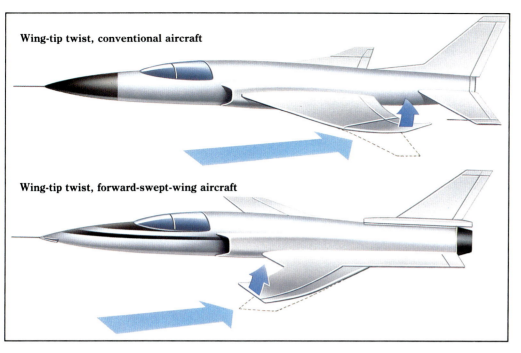

Wing-tip twist, conventional aircraft

Wing-tip twist, forward-swept-wing aircraft

Wing-tip twist

The X-29A's forward-swept wings increase lift and maneuverability. In addition to their unique design, this plane's wings are notable for their carbon-epoxy composite construction. Conventional wings made from metal alloys are flexible and sometimes give way under the strain of maneuvers. Wing-tip twist can damage and even destroy the wings. But the X-29A's composite wings are extremely stiff, enabling them to withstand the stress of demanding maneuvers.

Airflow and wing direction

Forward-swept wings produce an outboard-to-inboard airflow that reduces the likelihood of stalls. Though the X-29A is less stable than conventional aircraft, it is highly maneuverable at low speeds.

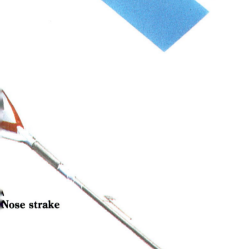

Airflow outboard to inboard

Nose strake

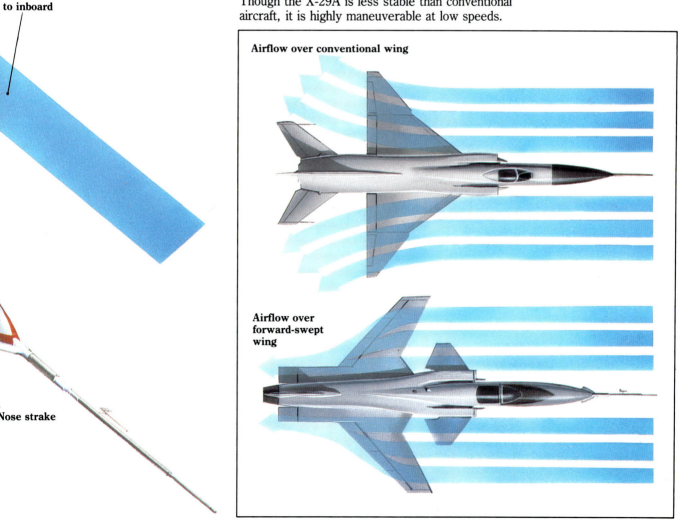

Airflow over conventional wing

Airflow over forward-swept wing

What Is a Stealth Aircraft?

Combat aircraft designers have long wanted to create a craft that was invisible to enemy radar. The American B-2 Stealth bomber, developed in the 1980s, was designed to evade detection by absorbing, rather than reflecting, radar waves. Constructed of special nonmetallic materials that are poor reflectors of radar waves, the B-2 also has a low-profile design with few projections, so that radar waves pass over and around the plane with little interception of the waves.

Aircraft can also be detected with infrared devices that sense heat from the engine exhausts. Stealth aircraft are designed to shield their exhaust heat, presenting a minimal infrared "signature." As a result, the highly secret B-2 Stealth bomber is very hard to detect, although not completely invisible.

Evading detection by radar

A Stealth aircraft's surface is covered with a patchwork of special radar-absorbing material. Incoming radar transmissions are split into two opposing waves that counteract each other, while the surface material converts the waves to heat energy, which is absorbed.

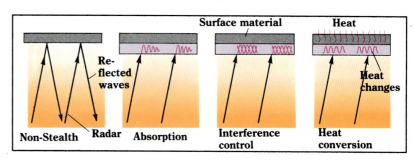

Surface material — Heat — Heat changes — Reflected waves — Non-Stealth — Radar — Absorption — Interference control — Heat conversion

The B-2 Stealth

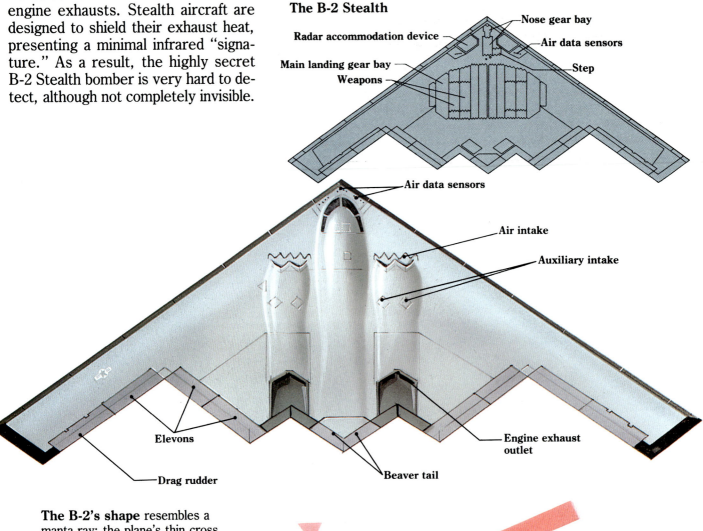

Radar accommodation device — Nose gear bay — Air data sensors — Main landing gear bay — Step — Weapons — Air data sensors — Air intake — Auxiliary intake — Elevons — Engine exhaust outlet — Drag rudder — Beaver tail

The B-2's shape resembles a manta ray; the plane's thin cross section presents a minimal target area for radar waves.

The B-2's special coating material cancels and absorbs radar waves. The aircraft's image on a radar screen is said to resemble nothing more than a large bird.

Glossary

Accelerator: A device, usually a pedal, for varying the speed of a vehicle by changing the amount of fuel fed to the engine.

Accelerometer: An instrument for measuring the acceleration of an aircraft.

Airfoil: Any surface, such as a wing, aileron, or stabilizer, designed to aid in lifting or controlling an aircraft by making use of the surrounding air currents.

Altimeter: A device used to find a plane's distance above sea level or other terrain.

Aneroid: A thin-walled, airtight compartment with an elastic lid that responds in a predictable way to changes in atmospheric pressure.

Axial compressor: A device that draws air into an engine and compresses it.

Axle: A shaft upon which wheels are mounted.

Bathyscaphe: A navigable, submersible vessel for exploring the depths of the ocean.

Bathysphere: A spherical diving apparatus used to study deep-sea life, lowered into the ocean by a cable.

Bearing: A supporting device that reduces friction between a stationary and a rotating part or between two moving parts.

Beaver tail: A control surface that combines with elevons to adjust the attitude and ensure the stability of an aircraft.

Brake cylinder: A metallic cylinder in a car or locomotive containing a piston that is forced outward to apply the brakes.

Brake shoe: A block of material formed to fit the curved surface of a car's drum or a train's wheel when braking.

Cam: A disk or cylinder with an irregular form whose motion gives the parts in contact with it a specific rocking action.

Canard: A device mounted at the front of a vehicle that acts as a stabilizer, or one of the two small lifting wings located in front of the main wings on some airplanes.

Carburetor: A device for mixing gasoline and air and delivering the mixture to cylinders.

Chassis: The frame, wheels, and machinery of an automobile.

Clutch: A rotating assembly for smoothly connecting and disconnecting engine power flow to the transmission.

Collective pitch lever: A lever used to control the angle of the blades of a helicopter rotor in unison to increase or decrease lift.

Combustion chamber: In an internal-combustion engine, the space inside the cylinder head and above the piston in which the fuel is burned.

Combustor: The apparatus in a jet engine for starting and sustaining combustion.

Compressor: A pump or other mechanism for reducing the volume and increasing the pressure of gases.

Condenser: A device for accumulating and holding a charge of electricity; also called a capacitor.

Control rod: A neutron-absorbing material that can be moved into or out of the core of a nuclear reactor to control the rate of fission.

Converter: A device that converts electrical energy from alternating current (AC) to direct current (DC) or vice versa.

Crankshaft: The main shaft of an engine; it converts the linear motion of the pistons to the rotary motion required to turn the drive shaft.

Cyclic pitch lever: A lever used to control a helicopter's horizontal movements by tilting the rotor blades to the right or left.

Cylinder: A cylindrical chamber in an engine block in which a piston operates.

Delta wing: A triangular surface that serves as both wing and horizontal stabilizer on space vehicles and on some supersonic aircraft.

Disc brake: A brake that operates by the friction of a caliper pressing pads against the sides of a rotating disc.

Dog clutch: A clutch used in vehicles with optional four-wheel drive in which the projections of one of the engaging parts fit into the recesses of the other, locking them together.

Drag: The aerodynamic force that tends to reduce the forward motion of an airfoil, airplane, or other aerodynamic body.

Electrode: A conductor through which an electric current enters or leaves a nonmetallic medium.

Electromagnet: A device in which an iron or steel core is magnetized by the electrical current in a surrounding coil.

Elevon: A control surface that functions both as an elevator and as an aileron.

Flange: A projecting rim for keeping an object in place.

Flap: A movable surface used for increasing the lift or drag on an airplane; or a surface used on high-speed automobiles to reduce the car's air resistance.

Flying bridge: A small, often open deck above a ship's pilothouse having duplicate controls and navigational equipment.

Foil: An airfoil or hydrofoil.

Forecastle: A structure at or immediately behind the bow of a vessel, used as a shelter for stores or machinery, or as quarters for sailors.

Fuselage: The complete central structure to which an airplane's wing, tail, and engines are attached.

Generator: A machine that converts mechanical energy into electrical energy.

Gimbal: A device that suspends an object in such a way that it will remain horizontal even when its support is tipped.

Gripman: A worker on a cable car who operates the device—called a grip—that starts or stops the car.

Gyrocompass: A navigational compass, containing a gyroscope, that automatically indicates true north.

Gyroscope: An apparatus that can maintain the same absolute direction in spite of the motion of its mountings and the surrounding parts.

Heat exchanger: The device in a nuclear reactor that uses heat generated by the nuclear reaction to boil water into steam, creating electrical energy.

Hertz (Hz): A unit of frequency, used to measure radio waves, equal to one cycle per second; kHz (kilohertz) is equal to one thousand cycles per second, and MHz (megahertz) is equal to one million cycles per second.

Hydrofoil: A winglike projection that lifts the hull of a moving vessel out of the water and generates thrust to propel the vessel.

Hydrostatic: Relating to the equilibrium and pressure of fluids.

Ignition coil: A set of coiled wires in an ignition system that increases the voltage delivered from the battery to the spark plugs.

Inducer: In a hydrofoil, the part of the waterjet pump that increases the speed of the water entering the pump and forces it through a nozzle to provide thrust.

Integrator: A navigational device used in aircraft that coordinates the information from the plane's accelerometers with time passed in order to calculate the plane's speed.

Inverter: A device that converts direct current (DC) into alternating current (AC).

Isopressure valve: A valve used in fire engines with foam sprayers that keeps the pressure of the liquids at constant levels.

Lift: The force exerted by the air that keeps an aircraft aloft.

Lifter: A small cylindrical device that connects a cam to a piston valve, controlling whether the valve is open or closed.

Light-emitting diode (LED): A semiconductor device that turns on a light when electric current passes through it.

Live steam: Steam direct from the boiler and at full pressure, ready for use.

Mach: A number indicating the ratio of an object's speed to the speed of sound; *mach 1* is equal to the speed of sound.

Manometer: An instrument for measuring the pressure of a fluid.

Pantograph: A device for transferring current from an overhead wire to a vehicle such as a trolley or an electric locomotive.

Pinion: A gear designed to mesh with a larger wheel, or a toothed shaft that engages a gear.

Piston: A disk or cylinder that moves within a tight-fitting sheath.

Piston rod: A rod that transfers a piston's motion to a connecting rod.

Pitch: The tilting of an aircraft's nose up or down, the angle at which a propeller blade is positioned on its hub, or the front-to-back rocking motion of a vessel.

Pitot tube: An instrument for measuring airspeed.

Pivot lock: A device that automatically locks contact couplings when the coupler heads meet.

Poop deck: The deck on top of the superstructure at the stern of a vessel.

Poppet valve: A valve that controls the intake and exhaust passages to the combustion chamber in most automobile engines.

Power cylinder: A hydraulic, computer-controlled device in a four-wheel steering system that moves the front or rear wheels to the left or right.

Radar: A device that projects an image of surrounding objects on a screen, determining their location by emitting a radio wave and then measuring the amount of time it takes for the echo to return.

Reactor: An apparatus in which a nuclear fission chain reaction can be started, sustained, and controlled to produce heat or useful radiation.

Revolutions per minute (rpm): A measurement of engine speed determined by the number of revolutions a crankshaft makes in one minute.

Ring gear: A gear that surrounds the planetary and sun gears in an automatic transmission.

Roll: The rotation of an airplane about the axis of the fuselage with little loss of altitude, or the side-to-side rocking motion of a vessel.

Rotor: The rotating part of a machine. In a car's electrical system, an electromagnet that rotates within the stator to supply the car with electricity; in an automatic transmission, part of the torque converter; in aircraft, a system of rotating airfoils such as the horizontal blades on a helicopter.

Rudder: On ships, a vertical blade at the stern of a vessel that can be turned to steer the vessel; on planes, a control surface attached to the vertical stabilizer and used, with the ailerons, to steer the plane.

Sink: A device that collects or dissipates electricity.

Sonar: A device for locating objects submerged in water by determining the amount of time it takes for an echo to return from the object.

Spoiler: An air deflector attached to an automobile, especially a racing car, to prevent the car from lifting off the road and to increase traction at high speeds; or a long, narrow plate along the top of an aircraft's wing used to reduce lift and increase drag.

Sponson: A flotation device used for landing an aircraft on water; it also stores fuel.

Stabilizer: On ships, a mechanical device for counteracting the roll of a vessel; on airplanes, a device for keeping an aircraft steady during flight.

Static tube: A tube that measures the pressure of a static—or motionless—fluid.

Stator: A stationary part in a machine in or about which a rotor revolves.

Strake: A horizontal control surface used on some aircraft to help the canards in climbing or descending.

Substation: An auxiliary power station where electric current is converted or where voltage is increased or decreased.

Superstructure: A part of a ship built on or above the main hull.

Suspender ring: A ring that connects the release lever to the head in a knuckle-type coupling.

Suspension: The system of springs and other devices that supports the frame and body of a vehicle from the axles.

Switching unit: A device used in electric cars for interrupting an electric circuit to prevent excessive current from damaging the circuit or causing a fire.

Synchronizer: A device in a transmission that causes meshing gears to move at the same rate in order to avoid gear clash.

Throttle: A mechanism that controls the flow of the air-fuel mixture to the cylinders.

Tongue rail: A movable rail that is shifted when a locomotive or car switches tracks.

Transfer gear: A transmission and differential assembly enclosed in a single housing.

Trim tank: A water tank that can be filled or emptied to ensure that a ship sits well in the water.

Turbine: Any of various machines having a rotor, usually with vanes or blades, driven by the pressure of a moving fluid such as water, steam, or air.

Ultrahigh frequency (UHF): Any frequency of radio waves between 300 and 3000 MHz.

Very high frequency (VHF): Any frequency of radio waves between 30 and 300 MHz.

Winch: A powerful machine with one or more drums on which to coil a rope, cable, or chain for hauling or lifting.

Yaw: To shift temporarily from a straight course.

Index

Staff for
UNDERSTANDING SCIENCE & NATURE

Assistant Managing Editor: Patricia Daniels
Editorial Directors: Allan Fallow, Karin Kinney
Writer: Mark Galan
Assistant Editor/Research: Elizabeth Thompson
Editorial Assistants: Louisa Potter, Marike van der Veen
Production Manager: Prudence G. Harris
Senior Copy Coordinator: Juli Duncan
Production: Celia Beattie
Library: Louise D. Forstall
Computer Composition: Deborah G. Tait (Manager), Monika D. Thayer, Janet Barnes Syring, Lillian Daniels

Special Contributors, Text: Joseph Alper, John Clausen, Margery duMond, Gina Maranto, Mark Washburn
Design: Antonio Alcalá, Nicholas Fasciano, David Neal Wiseman
Illustration/Photography: Cover: Stephen R. Wagner. 1: U.S. Coast Guard. 7: Association of American Railroads. 10: Art by Al Kettler. 13: Washington Metropolitan Area Transit Authority, photo by Larry Levine. 24: Washington Metropolitan Area Transit Authority, photo by Phil Portlock. 27: Washington Metropolitan Area Transit Authority, photo by Phil Portlock (top right). 29: Intamin Co. 30: Courtesy of San Francisco Convention and Visitors Bureau (top right). 33: JR-TOKAI, Central Japan Railway Company (top); GEC Alsthom/Bombardier (bottom left). 34-35: Art by Stephen Wagner; photo courtesy Thyssen Henschel, Kassel, Germany. 63: Michael Shelton/Cal Poly Pomona University (bottom right). 65: Destiny 2000 by Solar Electric, Santa Rosa, Calif. 70: Fairfax County Fire & Rescue Department. 75: Ingersoll-Rand (bottom right, 2). 77: Koehring Cranes and Excavators, Waverly, Iowa (top). 99: U.S. Navy (DN-ST-82-03869, DN-ST-89-01402, DN-ST-82-01350). 103: U.S. Navy (DN-ST-90-07857). 107: USAir. 116: The Goodyear Tire & Rubber Company (top). 125: Courtesy United Airlines (bottom).
Research: Robin Tunnicliff
Index: Barbara L. Klein

Consultants:
Anne Bennoff, Association of American Railroads; Cliff Black, Amtrak; Alex Campbell, Solar Electric; Robert J. Casey, President, High Speed Rail/Maglev Association; Cynthia Cecil, Intamin Co.; Al Cleeland, Ingersoll-Rand; Nicolas Finck, San Francisco Municipal Railway; Willis R. Goldschmidt, Museum of Transportation; Randy Gordee, Koehring, George Green, Koehring; Al Hixenbaugh, Boeing; Terry Kehoe, Kent Lester, Mark Lester, Supertrax International, Ontario; Russell E. Lee, Curator, Aeronautics Department, National Air and Space Museum, Smithsonian Institution; Larry Levine, Washington Metropolitan Area Transit Authority; Mark Messersmith, Ride & Show Engineering, Inc.; John T. Nansen, Museum of Transportation; Debo Ogunrinde, Washington Metropolitan Area Transit Authority; Gary Pope, Fairfax County Fire and Rescue; Michael D. Sakahara; Tina Shelton, Cal Poly Pomona; Russell Taylor.

TIME-LIFE for CHILDREN ®

President: Robert H. Smith
Associate Publisher and Managing Editor: Neil Kagan
Assistant Managing Editor: Patricia Daniels
Editorial Directors: Jean Burke Crawford, Allan Fallow, Karin Kinney, Sara Mark, Elizabeth Ward
Director of Marketing: Margaret Mooney
Product Managers: Cassandra Ford, Amy Haworth, Shelley L. Schimkus
Director of Finance: Lisa Peterson
Financial Analyst: Patricia Vanderslice
Publishing Assistant: Marike van der Veen
Administrative Assistant: Barbara A. Jones

Original English translation by International Editorial Services Inc./ C. E. Berry

First printing. Printed in U.S.A.
Published simultaneously in Canada.
Time Life Inc. is a wholly owned subsidiary of
THE TIME INC. BOOK COMPANY.
TIME-LIFE is a trademark of Time Warner Inc. U.S.A.
For subscription information, call 1-800-621-7026.

Library of Congress Cataloging-in-Publication Data
Transportation/ editors of Time-Life Books
       p.   cm. — (Understanding science & nature)
   Includes index.
   Summary: Questions and answers explore various aspects of transportation, including railroads, automobiles, ships, aircraft, and special purpose vehicles.
   ISBN 0-8094-9700-X (trade)
   ISBN 0-8094-9701-8 (lib.)
   1. Transportation—Juvenile literature.
   [1. Transportation—Miscellanea.
   2. Questions and answers.]
   I. Time-Life Books.   II. Series.
   TA1149.T73   1992
   629.04—dc20   92-24929
                                          CIP
                                          AC